MASTER YOUR THINKING

The Ultimate Guide to Empath Healing and to Stop Negative Thinking. Improve Your Emotional Intelligence with Self Esteem. Master Your Emotions and Improve Decision Making

By Jon Power

Summary

INTRODUCTION

You are an absolutely good person. You deserve a beautiful life, full of achievement, joy, happiness and enthusiasm. You have the right to have happy relationships, excellent health, meaningful work and freedom from capital. These are your birthright. That is what is supposed to happen in your life.

You are built to excel and have high levels of self-esteem, self-respect and personal pride. You are extraordinary; in all of mankind's history on earth, there has never been someone just like you. You have absolutely amazing untapped talents and abilities which can get you everything you might ever want in life when fully released and implemented.

You live in the greatest moment of all human history. You are surrounded by plenty of opportunities to make the most of and fulfill your goals. The only true limits on what you can, do, or have are the limitations that your own perception imposes upon yourself. Your future is practically boundless.

How did you react to the three paragraphs? You probably got two reactions. First of all, you loved what they said and your dearest wish was that they were valid for you. Yet, possibly, your second answer was one of cynicism and denial. Even though you sincerely wish to lead a perfectly safe, happy, prosperous life, your worries and fears emerged instantly as you read those words to remind you why these hopes and aspirations might not be possible for you.

Perhaps the most important mental and spiritual concept ever learned is that most of the time you become what you believe. The outside universe is a mirror image of your inner world. What's happening outside of you is a snapshot of what's going on inside. You can tell a person's inner state by looking at his or her life's outer circumstances. And it can't be any other way.

Your mind is incredibly powerful. Your emotions influence almost everything that happens to you, and decide everything. You can raise or lower your heart rate, boost or interfere with your metabolism, change your blood's chemical composition and help you sleep or stay awake at night.

You will make your feelings happy or sad, sometimes in a moment. You will warn you and make you conscious, or tired and distressed. They will make you popular or infamous, positive or negative, comfortable or nervous. You may feel powerful or weak in your mind, a survivor or a victor, a hero or a coward.

Your thoughts will make you a winner or a disappointment in your material life, wealthy or poverty-stricken, valued or forgotten. Your emotions, and the actions they cause, form your entire life. And the best news of all is they're totally under your own guidance.

You are a dynamic package of emotions, feelings, behaviors, expectations, pictures, worries, aspirations, concerns, beliefs and goals, often changing constantly, sometimes from second to second. Each of these factors influences the others in your temperament, sometimes in unpredictable ways. The whole of your life is the product of these variables intertwining and interconnecting.

The words and photos activate the feelings, and the emotions that go with them. Such images and feelings are causing actions and attitudes. Then your actions have consequences and outcomes which decide what's happening to you.

When you think about performance and confidence, you're going to feel confident and comfortable and you're going to perform well at whatever you do. If you're thinking about making mistakes or being humiliated you're going to perform badly, no matter how good you are.

From your imagination or from the external influences, pictures and photographs generate thoughts, feelings and actions that relate to them. We then cause acts that yield those consequences and tests. A person's thinking or circumstance can immediately cause you to feel happy or sad, elated or furious, caring or lonely.

Positive or negative, constructive or destructive, your behaviors contribute to the resulting images, feelings and actions that affect your life and relations. In turn, your behaviors are based on your previous experiences, and your simple assumptions on how life should be.

The feelings and perceptions that come with them are caused by your actions. You should actually act your way into emotion in a manner consistent with the conduct, by the Law of Reversibility. Through behaving as if you're always healthy, positive and confident, you'll soon start feeling that way inside. So your behaviors are completely under your influence, although your feelings are not.

The exterior dimensions of your life are good, in and of themselves. Only the sense you offer them defines your beliefs, thoughts, feelings and reactions to them. When you change your perspective about any part of your life, the way you feel and respond in that area will change. And since you can only decide what to do, you have the capacity to take complete control of your life.

The Law of Attraction states you are a "moving magnet" and inevitably draw the people, ideas, incentives and situations in accordance with your prevailing thoughts into your life.

If you think about hopeful, happy, caring and productive feelings, you generate a magnetism force field that draws the very things you're talking about, like iron filings to a magnet. This rule explains that it is you don't have to think about where the success can come from. If you can keep your mind clearly focused on what you want and refrain from worrying about what you don't want, just when you're ready you'll receive everything you need to achieve your goals. Shift your feelings, and change your life.

Successful people are the ones who think more creatively than people who have failed. We have different approaches to their lives, relationships, aspirations, challenges and experiences than others. We sow better plants, and we reap happier lives as a result. When you learn to think and act like other people who are successful, happy, wealthy, and prosperous, you will soon love the kind of life they are doing. You change your life because you change your own mindset.

CHAPTER 1

WHAT'S HEALTHY THINKING, AND WHY DOES IT MATTER?

It's possible you've thought at many times in your life that you might have a different, more optimistic outlook on things. This is a great example of wishful thinking, scolding yourself emotionally but not doing anything to consciously alter or remove those patterns that you so detest— that's a thought pit, a classic one that we'll explore later. At any point, before we get into the principles of thought loops and how good thinking impacts different types of people, we first have to ask the question: What is healthy thinking?

Yeah, in the literal sense, we can put together what it means — healthy living is thought in a manner that is good. But what does that mean in the light of our self-doubt, our pessimism that, for some, is like a virus that they don't seem to get rid of entirely. Leeching off their energies and what their motivation would be, negative thought is the leading cause of suicidal thinking, whether this pessimism is subconscious or deliberate. Pessimism can be a difficult and complex topic to discuss in and of itself, one that we will tackle later with thought loops and where they start.

What good thinking is, to be more precise, is the act of clearing your logical mind, which is reinforced by guilt, thinking that is only irrational and not rational at all, and reflecting on the truth of a situation at hand. If that fact means you have to look at something in a negative light, then so be it, as long as it's as objective as possible.

As people, we have this kind of tendency to be as truthful and as right as possible whenever we are able to be. That being said, you have to recognize that you can never be truly objective when pursuing the task of becoming a better person. While we would all love to think that we can become the supreme impartial authority, our perspectives are formed by our history and our perceptions, as well as our genetics— to some extent— as so, no matter how unbiased and rational we seek to be, there will always be a bit of our perspective that bends towards one thing or another because of our individual tastes and past experiences.

That's not to say the more rational and practical plan is of course fruitless. If only you were to live your life clouded by your thoughts, just travel through life in spur after a moment's spur, simply acting on the whim of your desires, you'd probably live an unfulfilled life. Living your life by justification alone will therefore always lead to a similar conclusion, so the best course is, like so many things, the middle way between those two extremes. It's impossible not to be subtly drawn in one direction or another, and it's likely to be on the side of sentiment or logic, but what counts is the effort to be as neutral as possible considering the position. Note, however, that the object of trying to remain impartial is not so that you can be objective and apathetic to things— the point of not wanting to be influenced by intense emotion or logic is keeping you satisfied and happy as an individual.

How good thinking always means is to identify the shortcomings in your thought, and to fix those flaws while maintaining modesty and trust. It can sometimes be disheartening to have flaws in your thought pointed out to you vigorously, but it is the development that follows after that feedback that matters more than the criticism itself. It's the desire to change and become a better person that far outweighs whatever guilt you may feel when you're attacked. It's rough, sure, but it does help a lot more than it hurts.

Now, another question arises from the first — sure, positive thought seeks to become a more neutral person for the sake of inner peace, but why does that matter to any person? If I am as good as it is, then why should I worry about safe thinking?

As one thing, if you assume that your attitude is as safe and optimistic as it is, you certainly wouldn't be reading this book at all. There's also a question that comes with positivity though. As I said, the best road with many issues is the one put in the midst of two extremes. On the one hand, we sometimes think about how damaging pessimism can be for the ego and for the self as a whole, but the risks of being too positive are a matter not nearly as debated. This is also a problem that we will discuss in later chapters, but for now bear in mind that any drastic in this sense is definitely one that will emotionally hurt you in the long run.

Anyway— why does logical reasoning matter? This is a question raised by those who are either happy with themselves or those who know their way of thought is deeply faulty, but who are either too prideful or too apathetic to take that first step forward and really be involved in your own improvement.

The fact is, positive thought isn't just intended for those who thinks their behavior is too dangerous, or whose thinking has the potential to ruin them from within. Yes, positive thinking is something that can help everyone and anyone at all, irrespective of how much you believe your mind is already in "good" form, or at least not so bad that you need to read a book on how to develop it.

The brain is probably the most laborious organ in your body. It not only succeeds in making us into living, alien creatures that can communicate and breathe and eat and create communities, but it also helps us to think. Our minds not only allow us to be conscious of our own thinking processes. To some level, anyway, we grasp our own thinking processes — and are able to analyze them, break them down and make them better. Our minds cause us to be so complex creatures that we are not at Mother Nature's whim or fate to make us better, or to teach us lessons about life. We have our own ability to tell ourselves knowledge, absorb the wisdom and apply it to every aspect of our lives. This is an insane thing to think of; our brain's power, but in the first place it is that same power that helps us to think about it.

Therefore, the strength of positive thought is really the same power our brain provides us— the ability to be aware and edit ourselves anytime you really want. The strength is something that we still take for granted, assuring ourselves that our religion, or destiny, will bring us on through life and that we don't really have to rely on our own thoughts to do much. We believe that we focus much, much less, on our feelings than we really do. The emotions are not only an integral part of us as humans, but that is what makes up the meaning, our constant stream of knowledge. The only moment in our minds when we feel "silence" is when we're so focused on something that all of our emotions go on the back burner for a while. We have an almost constant stream of internal expression running into our minds for the rest of our human experience, feeding us information that perhaps we didn't even know we had access to in the first place. Some of the emotions that we hear, some of them are not yet ours. Whether those are mischievous intrusive thoughts, or just thoughts we don't really agree with, spontaneous strings of knowledge that were more impulsive and intentional, those thoughts can sometimes trigger confusion in ourselves and in our own feelings. This discord between us and our emotions that causes a divide between our physical selves and our emotional selves can be extremely problematic when it comes to communicating more closely with ourselves, our beliefs or even sharing heart-to-heart relationships with other people. When we have a poor connection with ourselves, such relations can be weakened or strained. Healthy thought can both help to make a bond better and avoid the issues that can in the first place trigger the destructive fracture.

As you can see, positive thinking is something which in many ways affects us all. It's something that can have a tremendous effect on how we perceive the world around us, how we communicate with other individuals, and it's something that has the incredible power to turn our view of the world crazy.

Getting able to think well is, so to speak, getting able to take a step back. It's the potential that we each have in all of us to take a deeper look at ourselves — a look that can simultaneously be both harshly critical and soberingly rational. Looking at things like this encourages us to act on our impulses rather than just sitting around and dwelling on them, saying to ourselves that we should act instead of waking up and taking the action. It's those same positive thoughts that not only set our plans into action but keep those plans going, keep us engaged, keep us effective, and most of all, keep us happy as well as safe.

WHAT IS ANALYTICAL THINKING?

Analytical thinking is analyzing and examining an issue or subject for the creation of more complex ideas on it. Your analytical thinking can give rise to new insights, approaches or ideas related to the issue or topic.

The process usually includes multiple steps:

- Identifying a subject, question or concern
- Collecting facts
- Developing approaches or furthering the comprehension of the situation
- Checking solutions or new ideas based on what you have heard
- Post-analysis, or evaluating what solutions succeeded, or testing your new knowledge A key element of analytical thinking is the ability to quickly find triggers This means, for example, understanding what could happen during the problem-solving process and exploring how new ideas apply to the original topic.

The bulk of analytical thinking includes both trial and error. Those with good analytical thinking skills are often able to analyze a scenario, subject or problem easily and often work well within a team setting to achieve goals.

Why are analytical skills important?

Analytical skills are important as they help you to find solutions to common issues and to determine what actions to take next. Knowing situations and evaluating the scenario for viable solutions is a crucial competency at all rates in every role. Developing this skill will improve your job, help you achieve client goals and eventually promote your personal career objectives.

If you're looking for a specific job for analytics, such as a data analyst or laboratory analyst, you should develop your industry-specific analytical thinking skills. Although analytical thinking is a soft ability, analyst positions will also allow you to have specific hard competencies relevant to the profession. This also refers to professions with the technical knowledge required such as teaching, engineering, or scientific research.

Many other professions, including computer programming, engineering, education, and customer service, include using analytical skills on a regular basis.

How to improve your analytical skills

Improving your analytical skills could help you achieve different career goals. Increasing your analytical skills on your curriculum vitae and during your interview can also help you stand out in the hiring process when applying for jobs.

Consider taking a few of the following steps to improve your analytical skills:

- Taking on leadership roles requiring the use of critical analytical skills
- Develop essential analytical skills in your current role
- Take courses emphasizing the use of analytical skills
- Participate in events involving the use of analytical skills such as team sports, gaming or reading
- Seek advice or mentoring from experts in your field or business
- Provide work on best practices for your industry
- Improve your understanding of subject matter, which is necessary for better problem-solving

Take some time to evaluate the analytical skills that you possess and those where you can develop. Write down specific times when you used analytical skills to improve something or solve a problem, whether at work, in a volunteer position or at school.

WHAT IS EGO?

The ego is our own creation identity of the soul, an identification which is false. We're more than just attitude. If we take all of the assumptions about what we are— beliefs about our personalities, strengths, and abilities— we have our ego structure. Such skills, strengths and facets of our personalities will be characteristics of our skill, but our "self" intellectual model is false. And while this definition may seem like a stagnant thing to the ego, it is not. Actually, it is an integral and complex aspect of our personality, playing an important role in our lives to generate emotional drama.

The Ego Unmasked

Why is that ego too difficult to explain or describe? The ego is hard to define, because the ego is not one particular thing. In reality, it's made up of many different values a person acquires over their lifetime. Such beliefs may be complex and even conflicting. To confuse that further, the ego of each person is special. If someone defines and explains specifically all the aspects of their ego and what it pushes them to do, you may not get a good description of what it looks like. The challenge of becoming conscious of what your personal ego feels like is getting harder because our society does not praise us for turning our focus inward and realizing these issues.

How to Spot the Ego

The ego is hard to see, because it lies behind real-life perceptions—our adherence to representations of our personality—and because we haven't practiced searching. You can glimpse other feelings, similar to those mentioned above, by observing them. The easiest way to spot the ego is through the trail of emotional reactions that it leaves behind: frustration at a loved one, a need to be perfect, a sense of vulnerability in some cases, irrational feelings of envy, the need to please someone, and so on. The false beliefs that form the ego will relate these feelings to. In the beginning the signs of subsequent feelings and stress are harder to see, rather than the personality that triggered it.

One of the ego's most troubling characteristics is that it produces powerful emotional emotions, then excuses us for how it made us feel. The indignation with which we respond stems from ego-based assumptions that we are right and' know better' than someone else. There may also be an understanding of the survivor of deception or inequality below. When we overreact with frustration we can feel bad about what we've been saying. The ego is moving to a "righteous self" that "knows better" and is advising us to overreact with frustration. Simultaneously, it assumes the reputation of being the "stupid idiot" who knows no better and takes the blame for overreacting. All of these actions, emotions, and opinions take place in the subconscious, and although they are entirely different, we believe they many come from us. If they were words that really come from our own selves they wouldn't dispute and we could save them.

To the unconscious person, the distinction between what is ego and what it really is hard to discern. They're left to wonder, "What happened to me that I had behaved like this?" And their post-emotional examination lacks the understanding of treating the various parts of their system of beliefs at work as distinct from themselves. As a result, one of the accusing voices in their head blames everything that they say on "they themselves." The ego then hijacks the study and turns it into a process of self-criticism / blame. You have no chance to see the root cause of your interpersonal tragedies when the ego dominates the self-reflection process, as the ego reaffirms itself and hides in self-criticism.

Is the ego arrogant or insecure?

"Having an ego" is usually associated with pride, and is a term used to describe someone who feels that they are stronger than others. And that's just a function of the ego. It is actually possible to have some positive self-esteem and some negative self-esteem-at different times we are mindful of these different beliefs. The pessimistic views about our self-making make up our negative self-esteem, while our positive thoughts reflect our positive self-esteem. Together, our ego shapes the negative and the positive value.

Quite often, these two facets of our personalities are almost equal in size, and morally balance each other. A person with their inner critic who is very harsh on him or herself may have feelings of worthlessness. This is a difficult emotion to deal with, and they may cover it up with bravado to disguise the pain, projecting an image of stability and loyalty, all the while coping with feelings of insecurity, worthlessness and inadequacy.

Arrogance differs markedly from the belief that doesn't come from vanity. A person can have total confidence in his ability, ability, or self-acceptance, without making him "go to his head" and having an impact on his relationships with others. And while modesty can often be mistaken for shyness and vulnerability, a person of true humility is fully present and at peace with himself and his world. Confidence without pride, modesty without fear, these are personality habits which are without the ego's self-image dynamics.

Letting Go of the Ego

Since the ego has multiple aspects, dissolving all of it at once is not realistic or successful, nor is it possible you will. Just like a tree or big bush overgrown in the yard, you're not just taking it out and throwing it away—you're carving out useful bits instead. The same method is successful in letting go of the false convictions which make up the ego. You start by detaching yourself from individual thoughts which reinforce the ego, then letting go of beliefs, removing yourself from your ego's false identity.

We have spent years creating and strengthening our self-images of personality, working behind them. It will take more than a few days to remove our true selves from that web of false beliefs. Yeah, it'll take some time...... so what. Learning to read, do math, walk and develop skills at any useful activity always took a while. It takes time and practice to get things worth doing. What better thing to do than let go of what makes you unhappiness?

CHAPTER 2

THE SUMS OF OUR THOUGHTS

Our thoughts and feelings play a massive role in the everyday way in which we live our lives as individuals more than we so often know and document. After all, the very reason we wake up in the morning is determined by our first alert, conscious thoughts. Why we do the things we do, the path in life we take on the basis of those choices, and the places we end up in, are largely decided by our constant stream of thoughts that we have to choose through every day to figure out which thoughts we hope will enable us to excel that day and on. Each idea we have, although it may seem dismissible, is something that could have produced an infinite number of past decisions and emotions. Also impulsive feelings, and the ideas that we most hate— those that we hide deep within us and try to push away in the expectation that they will never emerge and lift their ugly heads — are thoughts and expressions of our personalities that we cannot disregard. Therefore, in the long run, we cannot neglect them and still be healthy people working. Most people have all sorts of ways of dealing with their feelings, many of which they may not like. Many people choose to record their thoughts in some manner, whether through a kind of video diary or written entries — this approach allows you to express your thoughts more concretely, which in effect will allow you to address these issues more effectively and with a better objective in mind. For fact, video diary entries, or any other kind of verbalization of concerns or intrusive feelings, help clear the mind of tension or other troubles. For example, there are so many ways people go about dealing with their feelings and their problems and some try to deal with those same thoughts by avoiding them and almost slipping into a denial state.

While for some people this state of denial can succeed, most of it for at least a short while, there are very few people who can really drive a string of thoughts away forever. There are not many people in the world who can block any kind of idea for a very long time— this may be why many people say a thought that is "true" or "fated" to see the light of day will still find its way out. Despite the fact that this statement is old and fairly ambiguous, experience has seen reality. Also, when we have something we talk about it upsets us, it's generally something disturbing because either it's true or it's connected to the truth. The fact with which we have not yet come to terms is that the truth which makes us the most uncomfortable — take, for example, Harper Lee's To Kill a Mockingbird. In early 20th century America, Lee's seminal novella of corruption, punishment, and racism is one that is heavily discussed, even today. It often tops the charts of literary works most commonly banned or written about in classrooms, most of those protests citing sexism, vocabulary of use or derogation or connection to violence as a purpose. Of course, many would say that the true reason Lee's masterpiece makes so many people so profoundly sad is because they all know, in a small part of themselves, that the book's preachings are still true for today. We have far from removing the problems so strongly touched on in the novel, and yet we now have something of a growing social problem in which one side disputes that we have eradicated the hate speech and the ignorance of people so antagonistically depicted, and the other side insists that we have not only removed the contentious and insulting subjects of the book more or less, but that the book's. The argument goes on and on as it has been for many years now, and will continue for many years, but the point that To Kill a Mockingbird and many other classic and divisive works of literature make is that the facts will always make people uncomfortable as long as that fact is one that embarrasses other people. Actually, humans are a fundamentally selfish race, doing virtually anything to satisfy their vanity, recover a weakened ego, and convince themselves and others that they are correct in any debate, regardless of the cost. Of course we want to be right by nature for happiness, pleasure, and often for recognition, from our colleagues and/or our subordinates. We both know how good it feels to be right and prove wrong if we can, to an annoying colleague. We also assume responsibility for those selfish things we do, and yet we love them. We understand what they mean about us but we should look at ourselves and judge our actions honestly and without delusion — at any rate, most of us.

Yet, what does all of this mean in the sense of balanced thinking? What that says, actually, is much easier than you might imagine. In a way, not only do our minds identify us as people but in exchange we also have the power to define our thoughts. While our emotions do have the ability to dominate our lives and our environment, we also have the same power to take hold of our own thoughts and manage them, rather than allowing them to rule us entirely. Taking control of your thoughts is quite straightforward, really— all you need to do is become self-aware to the extent where you keep up with your thoughts and feedback about those same thoughts in near real time.

The harsh truth is, we often either give ourselves too much, or too little, of the harsh truth. Actively mediating, and somehow trying to find the middle ground between the two nations, is very complicated. Each situation in which we take part, whether we are participating or simply watching on the sidelines, has a rather pronounced effect on what we do, what we say, how we behave and how we respond afterwards. Even if that occurrence is not actually extremely good or catastrophic, even the most ordinary incidents will, if only small, change the trajectory of the rest of our days. Even in the literal sense, we are affected by everything we do: spending a few extra minutes in the bathroom to contemplate the day ahead and the days ahead of you will then mean that you have less time to finish getting ready for your day, and those extra few minutes may actually end up making you late to whatever duty you may have had for that day. Even the little things that happen to us every day, you know, change the way we respond.

Of course, this also extends to more introspective situations, to more painful and gloomy situations that may involve more positive thought, emotion and healing. Imagine, you were in a car accident, for example — the collision was relatively low-speed, and no one was badly injured by the impact. Nonetheless, before starting your normal routine, you have had to take time to fully heal from the said incident. While you have, of course, had to take the time to heal emotionally from that accident, the lasting effects go far beyond the immediate. Regardless matter how long you take to heal your body, regardless matter how long it takes you to resolve the anxiety or discomfort that you may have formed of cars as a result of the incident, you probably won't always have a lasting impression, and you will change the way you react and behave when you drive, no matter how minute the shift may become over time. Also years and years later, when the accident is nothing but a remarkable recollection, it will have been an event that has forever changed the way you responded to danger on the road, how carefully you behaved while behind the wheel, and many other things in a vehicle, walking or whatever. Any kind of trauma such as this that you undergo, be it solely physical or psychological, will have a lasting impact on how you respond in the future in cases where the events are associated with your past experiences. It may become a blessing or a curse, but it is what happens, even in those with an exceptionally good memory. After all, the more you remember the incident, the more often you can remember the emotions during it. Of all those emotions that change the course of your life forever.

That does not have to be this way forever, of course. You don't just have to struggle passively while you let everything that happens around you slip you by and leave a scar you're not in charge of, but you don't have to take a back seat to your own feelings. In your thinking, you play a much more active role than you might actually think, or that it might seem. Not only are you able to control your emotions in a certain way, but you can also influence and control how you are influenced by those feelings. Of course, you'll certainly always have some idiosyncrasies that remain with you due to your past experiences, but how you view your stream of consciousness is up to you, more or less. Whether you let the perception of your emotions affect your decision forwards is up to you, based on how aware you really are of your feelings.

Self-awareness is something that most people find very difficult to do, mostly because you have to be relatively self-aware, to begin with, to establish a sense of self-awareness. In your day-to-day activities, being able to identify the wrong things in your life to seeking change and purpose can be the difference between living a fulfilling life and simply growing through the motions and wondering what you ever wanted to accomplish in your life. It's very hard to get the confidence to initiate the transition on its own, but I can honestly guarantee you that any risk you take will grow to be embraced not only by you, but by the people around you who matter for you and want good things for you. Such followers, whether they're your friends, relatives, and partner, or just a group of people online with whom you believe you're related, are likely to grow to be one of the, if not the, main driving forces behind the drive to be successful and to change your way of life and your mindset.

And yeah, it's hard to put better thinking into your everyday life. It is not only hard to get started, but it is also very difficult to keep going. You may get draining the inspiration and the energy you need to keep up, to keep pushing forward to improve the way you think, and the way you live. Only keep pushing, as it is with all things, while feeling the pressure to succeed. But — not as stressful as a life in which you exist only in the extremes, where you are always either positive and in denial or so gloomy that your perspective influences all aspects of your life. Yeah, learning how to hold your drive up for long periods of time is unbelievably difficult, but note, so to speak, that you'll have support in every corner of your ring. We'll explore the idea of "thought traps" in the next chapter —how they play in your everyday life, how you can repair them, and what they can do to you as a person on your way to changing your life and being happier and healthier.

HOW TO CHANGE YOUR THINKING

1. Change your thoughts by creating positive affirmations

Assurances aren't always optimistic. We too can be pessimistic. The hexes the witches make are pessimistic affirmations.

The reality is that most people are given pessimistic statements to make. If you constantly believe you won't be successful in a particular project, it's a pessimistic reinforcement. Affirmations, both negative and positive effects on brain neurological function.

Positive statements mimic mantras. We have a divine and holy energy about them. Let us be sure that constructive affirmations are made. We should not be low or prescriptive.

Thoughts like' shall," sought to' or' abstain from' are prescriptive.

Types of negative statements include:' I can't' do this. It's' pretty hard.' On the other, affirmations such as' I will," I should' or' I'm going to' should be strong and committed. As described above, your brain often adapts to your habits of thought, and commands your organs to act accordingly.

2. Learn to apply full stop

We keep mulling about our misfortunes, the supposed wrongs done to us by those we so deeply cherished and stood by. They never stop to blame ourselves for the errors they think we have made. And if I had done this or that, would have happened? What would happen in future if I were to do this or that?

This is not to say that we should not learn from past mistakes, or intelligently plan our future. The only thing we can stop thinking about once we've learned about our mistakes and settled on our future.

3. Let go of the need to be masochistic

We love to wallow in our suffering quite often. They enjoy creating self-punishing emotions or being gloomy and somber. Here's an example: "When I start selling candles, the sun will stop setting, people will stop dying when I start selling shrouds." I was born unfortunate. Something good happens to me ever.

Not only do these emotions have a negative effect on the psyche, but they also have an adverse effect on your physical health.

4. Change your thoughts by counting your joys and blessings

Many people take for granted their joys and riches and start grumbling about what they don't have; or when they are faced with challenges and troubles. Only speak of those less lucky than yourselves. Or, think of a situation which might have been worse than it is now. You weep because an injury has injured your leg. What, had the limb broken itself? For happiness see the full half of the bottle and the vacant half with a determination to fill it.

5. Appreciate and enjoy what you already have

Always understand and accept what you already have, is a perfect way to change your feelings. This is not to say you don't aspire to an even better life. Accept the amount of success you've gained, instead of feeling sad about what you couldn't do. Sometimes setting higher targets or goals is no mistake, but failure to reach them should not ruin the satisfaction of what you already have.

WHAT IS CRITICAL THINKING?

The ability to think logically and rationally, to grasp the logical connection between concepts, is critical thinking. Since the time of early Greek thinkers such as Plato and Socrates, critical thinking has been the subject of much debate and analysis and has continued to be a subject of discussion into modern age, such as the ability to recognize false news.

Critical thinking could be described as being capable of engaging in analytical, independent thought.

Critical thinking essentially requires you to make use of your abilities to reason. It's about being an active learner, rather than a passive learning receiver.

Critical thinkers challenge theories and conclusions rigorously, instead of taking them at face value. We will always try to decide whether the whole picture is reflected by concepts, claims and results and are open to finding that they do not.

Critical thinkers should objectively define, evaluate, and solve problems, rather than through intuition or instinct.

Someone who has critical thinking skills may:

- Consider the links between concepts.
- Determine the validity and value of the claims and ideas.
- Recognize, create and appraise claims.
- Identify inconsistencies and logic mistakes.
- Consistently and consistently resolve challenges.
- Think on why their own opinions, convictions and ideals are valid.

In certain cases, critical thinking involves thinking about things in order to arrive at the best possible solution in the situations which the thinker is aware of. It's a way of thinking about what's currently occupying your mind in more everyday language, so that you come to the best possible conclusion.

CHAPTER 3

THINKING TRAPS, OR THINKING "SANDPITS"

There are many situations in which all sorts of people can slip through conceptual traps, many of which are extremely difficult to navigate our way out of-difficult, but certainly not impossible. Nonetheless, there are a certain number of specific loopholes in which most individuals suffering persistent depression are often deeply entrenched. This article is by no means one that extends to all kinds of people, but it is a broad compilation of common "thought pits," and common ways to get out of them.

- Over generalizing a bad time — this kind of person is often a very fatalistic person, someone who has decided the worst result possible will always come to pass. When that result does not arrive, they completely ignore it, but when it does-this type of person frequently uses words like "still" and "never" to convey their belief that they are undergoing an endless cycle of horrible karma or something of that nature. This kind of person is susceptible to being influenced by the views of others about them but is also someone who is generally very direct with their own beliefs, often persuaded that opinions formed from other people's thoughts and emotions are in fact their original model. Often someone who is a pathological over generalizer often generalizes something too poorly because they want publicity or, put more simply, they want support. The theatrical style is often something like an appeal for help, an indication or desperation of a sense of helplessness they feel powerless to stop. We don't want to feel as helpless as they do sometimes, but they feel like they're always at the universe's mercy, never in control of their "fate." Like I said, they are inclined to being relatively fatalistic and are therefore never particularly inspired when it comes to shaping their fate or taking action to improve themselves — they usually feel that nothing they do is going to matter in the long run, so there is no great point in trying to do anything different when all will inevitably return to their original state. Someone who feels this kind of thought trap may feel compelled to merely lazily let themselves travel through life without any concern or connection in the universe, but they must wake up and realize that living that way would lead them to the road of unfulfillment and hollow existence. They have to be the first to get up and actually do something about it if they want to change their "life," their "destiny," their "fate"

Those who constantly generalize over also consider themselves the persistent beneficiary of terrible luck. I say such things like, "this always happens to me!" In the heart, some of these people know it's not logically true, so they tell it anyway because it gives them a form of cathartic relief to feel as if they can't change their situation in any way. People who fall into negative thinking of this type are typically unified by a feeling of being a survivor. The respect and affection they so desperately needed as children were obviously not given to them, and their need for attention reflects in this way. This is not, of course, always the way that this need for recognition appears in adults. Unfortunately, often children who have been abused in their history, either by their mother or by someone else in their earlier lives, demonstrate their need for affection and comfort by imagining themselves to be the victim of almost any situation in which they are. Those who generalize this way sometimes have a resemblance to pathological liars, thinking themselves to be the perpetrator, where they may be the abuser. We need to understand and document the fact that the world has no more or less regard for them than any other human on Earth in any way, shape or form. The belief or hypothesis that they actually receive bad luck more often than others, no matter how it may seem to them, is little more than paranoia. The only thing that affects how many good or bad things happen to them is the decisions they do for themselves, or do not. There is no karmic power which will turn your life around someday. You have to be the person standing up and pushing yourself to confront the reality of a situation. Whether that fact leans on the good or the negative side, there is hardly any better medicine for those who believe they have any specialties in the universe's eyes than a strong dose of humility. The modesty will at least do something to convince them the not only do they have no actual karmic power in the world that punishes them for some random act, but they are the only thing in the universe that can lead the active role in making their lives fulfilled.

- People who think of the world as wrong and right, black and white, yes or no — these kinds of people are the types of characters that are often too harsh on themselves, and sometimes too hard on others too. We are people who want to do well but are opposed to the idea that there is some sort of grey area between two ends of a situation for whatever reason. They want an answer to every and every question, a straightforward and definite answer that is transparent and lined up in dark red ink before them. We want to be replied, not just as a figure of authority or someone with influence, but just as someone who is on an almost continual quest for knowledge and comprehension of everything and anything. We want to explain in the easiest and clearest possible terms, all we can. Using "I don't know" for a reaction is usually very difficult for them, even tougher than using "no" It's the complexity of a situation that upsets them and drives them crazy to no end. I can't stand the thought that they don't know and cannot understand the way the cogs churn in everything. These are also the kinds of people that give themselves too barely the leeway. This kind of thought also derives from strain in their youth, where they were probably a child who, in college or some other area, excelled, or was pressured to excel. The pressure to succeed, pressure that so often came in very toxic doses, became so normal for them, that they simply adopted the coping mechanism for themselves in their adulthood. Today, the black and white thinker doesn't let themselves rest in their maturity, doesn't let themselves have a break from their potentially busy— and definitely overwhelmed with different tasks and responsibilities— life, and almost certainly doesn't let themselves indulge and have a weekend off. We always have to be employed, we always have to be successful and in their own eyes they are meaningless. This is undoubtedly how they were taught by their parents or guardians— so that they become valuable when they do excel and when they do become the strongest. Yet when they are no longer the best, or when they rest or unwind, they are worthless. This kind of intense thinking comes from an incomprehension that relaxing is a very important part of efficiency. They don't know how to relax because they grew up with the idea that it was infinitely more important to be successful than being healthy, confident or satisfied. They just take the "A+" as a grade when starting a program. If they are not immediately up to their own expectations, then the whole idea is a total disaster, they are a loser, and now the thinking is worth nothing for them. This is a very dangerous way of thinking as it often drives them to cancel plans as soon as they hit the first obstacle, no matter how long or complicated it may be. As long as there is any sign of potential danger, or the slightest hint of what may grow to be that they find a mistake, they are much more likely to abandon their scheme completely than others who do not share their mentality. This is an intense, often dysfunctional habit for many people, as you can see, and it often makes people seem less attractive as mates and as partners as well. Someone who views the world solely through a strictly black and white filter will be draining to the stomach for most people, and will therefore be less enjoyable to be around than others. Treating the universe as a science project not only pressures and dehumanizes the people around the individual, it also stresses them out and can lead to the loss of their sense of identity in many instances. A diminished identity may seem like the last expected result of viewing the world too negatively, but to put it this way may be more eloquent, more simply— we, as people, have an identity more or less determined by our emotions and experiences. If you do all you can to remove the "gray area" that feelings generate in contexts, and therefore restrict the cognitive capacity of your interactions to just the actual, realistic, surface-level interpretation, you will lack the credibility that your emotions once so carefully cultivated over time. Such types of people are best suited to conditions in which they are required to adapt, in terms of improvement. Someone who's generally too hard on themselves and others need to know how to find a balance and realize that they don't have to give into their intense compulsions. When they understand the dangers and long-term disadvantages that life can have in this manner, people who look at stuff like this are more likely to loosen up and take advice from others, as well as consider a touch of grey for every black and white human.

- The cynical fortuneteller— this is someone who's recognized for someone who's constantly forecasting the future, and who's always likely to blow in their face for that prediction. The fortune teller may take as many positive steps towards their target as they like, but they still find themselves falling prey to the voice in their head that warns them that no matter what, in all their efforts they are doomed to suffer a loss of a disappointment. Such kinds of forecasts frequently lack overwhelming facts, and yet they somehow find a way to twist virtually every story against them, even when they don't actually want to. This kind of person comes under the umbrella more or less that the over-generalizer is also frequently found under, as the two are very close in their defeatist attitude. The main difference between the two styles lies in the fact that while most people who over-generalize were once adolescents starved of love so that by victimizing themselves they are now finding some satisfaction, the fortuneteller doesn't necessarily seek that affirmation from others as much. Alternatively, fortunetellers respond as a child to a lack of attention and love by internalizing the disrespect. The over-generalizer thinks they have been mistaken by not being given the respect they feel they deserve, while the fortuneteller believes it is much more likely that they deserve the lack of recognition. By not being granted consideration they don't necessarily feel guilty, since they believe the injustice was warranted more than not. While the over-generalizer thinks terrible things are going to happen to them because they sound like the world is out to get them, the never-upbeat fortuneteller has a bad habit of always convincing himself they are always being set up for failure. The difference lies in where these two forms assume that the antagonism stems from. While the former kind firmly believes that there is some supernatural force that relentlessly sabotaging them and their dreams, the latter kind of individual is far more likely to believe that they are the ones who destroy themselves. This fortuneteller considers themselves to be someone who deserves their own misfortune, and they expect it to continue far into the future. Any bad thing that happens to them now only leads to their firm conviction that they are the perpetual victim of their own negative qualities. Not only that, but the cynical fortuneteller thinks they are disproportionately inferior to those around them, sometimes assuring themselves and sometimes even others that they really don't have what it takes to succeed in whatever they seek. We firmly believe we are destined to fail not because of the flaws in the cosmos or some divine fate, but because of their own shortcomings. Instead of generalizing the way things only "seem" to happen to them, they generalize their way of acting and behaving in order to paint themselves as useless. Like most styles on these lists, the fortuneteller almost always has a damagingly low self-esteem, and so seeking the emotional comfort they are hoping for extremely difficult. Occasionally, these people's best escape is just going to therapy and sorting out their problems with the help of a therapist who knows how to treat them. For example, if professional help is out of the picture— whether that is because the condition is not serious enough, or the person in question simply refuses to see a psychiatrist or some other form of approved aid— any strategies that often benefit people with a similar problematic problem include replacing the bad behavior with another. Occasionally, those who want to get rid of unwanted or uncomfortable mental tics or repetitive feelings, snap themselves with a rubber band or have some other kind of mind but not torturous physical punishment imposed on them, either by themselves or by another human, if they slip up and fall back into the habit. To many, this is an unorthodox approach but it certainly works well for most people. Alternatively, for those with the willpower, they can find positive affirmations that take the place of time that otherwise would be spent putting themselves down. For example, if you hear something like "I know I've done well, but I'll actually either mess up or lose somehow," contradict yourself— either out loud or to yourself— and say something positive to overcome the negative feeling. Even if it sounds slight or excessively stupid, and the positive feeling conveyed to you on a regular basis over a period of time will show results in your life and mind. Doing such things over and over again will increase your self-esteem and motivation over time. Of course, like all recovery, it's a slow process, but when you start experiencing life outside of your thought pit, whatever effort you have to do to live in that position becomes more than worth the trouble.

- Emotional reasoning — a completely different type of mental sandpit, and one that is just as unhealthy and dangerous, but for a whole different set of reasons. Simply put, emotional reasoners find a way to let their emotions— that is, their fears— take over their thinking, keeping them away from what could be a peaceful, safe environment. Most men, for starters, are afraid of heights, aircraft or the ocean. Persons who have this anxiety and an emotional thinking pattern may conclude that those areas are logically dangerous if they feel anxious when they are out on the beach, in an airport, or at a high place. This kind of thought can really hinder what a person can do, whether it means that they can make their travel plans unnecessarily long and boring, or never get a decent chance to enjoy the beach at all. People who think like this may also have a propensity to victimize themselves and thus often ruin other people's fun of things. It does not come from a very malevolent place, like all the other forms on those lists, but it comes from a buried desire place. Of course the need is for attention and care. Those who victimize themselves like that were always once young living in a household that had some sort of unspoken social code. We often have no way to vent their feelings, and fear adequately because they have never before been able to share them. So now that maturity encourages them to express their feelings, they have no idea how to reconcile their reasoning and their emotions. But, since they have such a negative connotation with using their logic and reasoning, it is often difficult to find a balance because people like this sometimes face difficulty in using their regular reasoning. That can make them feel like they have to use their emotions to make up for "lost time" at almost all times today. This habit may or may not be involuntary but it is a habit that affects many people in various ways. For simplicity's sake, I'm explaining all the different types of traps of thought and people who suffer from them in very drastic terms. Many people don't really feel this way about their feelings or their fears, but for a fairly long time this is something that lingers inside them. The way to get rid of this habitual emotional-logical paradox? Exposure therapy. Like many of the people who suffer from these loops of thought, emotional reasoners believe that there is some sort of bad spiral that is either triggered by or associated with those events that give them distress. Ideally, they need to be shown that these things aren't dangerous at all, and are just really fun when you can calm down and let yourself think your way out of the anxiety spiral. If they can finally feel comfortable in an environment where they would normally feel lots of stress and anxiety, the possibility of having to endure such problems will be more accessible to emotional reasoners. This also helps them to use their logic and reasoning, rather than just using their emotional response— their knee-jerk response— to anything that causes them discomfort or makes them uncomfortable. It will support an emotional reasoner, of course, to have a partner with them when they go through one of those stressful moments. Getting a close "voice of reason" will help them feel at home and practice their reasoning skills to get them out of their own heads.

- Negative labeling— these kinds of people are most commonly found in an office or high school today. Some kinds of people don't know how to get positive attention from others correctly, so they mark themselves outwardly as derogatory. Negative labelers, however, often have difficulty labeling those around them as simply their negative qualities. Simply put, the negative labeler is typically a person who has been unfairly branded throughout much of their life. Often we see that when used to them, people who view us unfairly and see the world in his kind of cut and paste, black and white lens were first introduced to that spectrum. Throughout their youth they were undoubtedly surrounded by people who looked at life in a similar manner, blaming others and themselves for their suffering, but doing nothing to personally try and stop it. That sort of laziness is also often only attributed to whoever they claim that way in their past actions. The aggressive labeler, as children so often do, just picks up where that person left off in their youth, acting the way they do because it's the only way they know how to handle these kinds of issues. Compared to the "black and white" form in section one, pessimistic labelers also have a tendency to see things in a very cut and dry way. Some people want things to go their way, or else the fault lies with little to no guilt either in the other side or themselves. We learn how to criticize themselves but not how to solve the problem by doing anything constructive about it. This happens in a lot of people— they have a kind of defeatist mentality, yet they do nothing to stand up and get actively involved in changing anything or making a better decision. We let it go until it comes back and hits them hard enough to drive them out of their chair because we believe they have done something wrong. To negative labelers a simple solution is to force them into being more positive about their lives. Since they take their own decisions so often with a back seat, they may not realize what it is like to take responsibility and repair it. The question also arises when people let their failures go after they let threats fly— when they do nothing to solve the problem, they not only let the problem go free, but they also let their relationships with others deteriorate when they do nothing to restore them.

Such people need a tough wake-up call, something bad to happen to them and someone to be up front with them, remind them that if they just corrected their initial mistake, such bad things wouldn't happen to them! What pessimistic labelers might assume is a relentless loop of negative events is really a cycle of events that sprang from their original fault, which will now come back and bite them over and over again. Negative labelers are individuals who, until something serious happens, are unable to do anything about their condition and what constitutes "bad" for them will vary from person to person.

- "Should have, could have, would have" statements— this kind of pit of thought happens mostly in individuals who are not opportunistic, but may wish they could be more like that. Those who often fall into this pit believe that they are inferior or that they do not reach their full potential because they do not deliver on their desires, yet they do not act on them. This sort of thought pit, somewhat similar to the derogatory labeling method, often does not necessarily inspire the person in question— it only drives them deeper and deeper into their hole of self-doubt, without motivating them to do anything about it. This is because not only does this kind of thought lock the individual into the illusion of what might have been and set them up for disappointment by setting their expectations far too high for themselves, but it also puts them in the frame of mind that they are helpless or too fragile to do the acts they desire, or say the things that are most on their minds. We believe we have to act in a certain way, that this is the only way to accomplish their goal, and they don't open their eyes to the rewards of what they did. People who fall into this trap of thinking usually have a lot of trouble letting go of the past and making peace with their choices, sometimes suffering from the sense that "grass is always greener," assuming their life would be different, and stronger if they had taken completely different decisions. Occasionally, they may or may not realize instinctively that this is simply not true, that it wouldn't change their present state at all, no matter what they had done in the past. Nonetheless, people who fall into this kind of trap of thinking, or pessimistic spiral of emotion, generally always feel anxious and discouraged about their own past choices. The best way to defeat this kind of reasoning is to push them to avoid thinking about the past, and their actions. Therefore, reflecting instead on the moment is the best way to counteracting the feelings of regret.

Instead of worrying only about the previous decisions they have made and the impact they have on them, they should focus their attention on the decisions they have immediately in front of them or near ahead. We also hyper-focus on the regrets of their life we have about past decisions, when instead they could focus on bringing more consideration and careful deliberation into their management decisions. If you concentrate on the things that you can influence, you will end up with significantly fewer regrets in the future. Positive affirmations often support when faced with regret and sadness about a choice that you may have felt was taken in poor taste. Even though you can't change the decision you've made in the past, there are always ways you can overcome the change you've made in your and other lifetimes. Not only can you focus on making better choices from now on, but you can also try to correct the effects that your bad choices have made on your life and on others' lives. Showing you want to improve will not only allow others to forgive you, but will also support you to form relationships that you may have missed from those bad choices. In fact, for those who struggle from this sort of remorse, keep in mind that although your choices are irreversible and cannot be reversed in and of themselves, you have the power to control where you ultimately take those decisions. You can monitor how you respond to circumstances that throw your way, and you have the power to change your life course even more than you might expect.

- Mind reader— this type of person is often, somehow, incredibly confident and nervous at the same time. People seem to have such incredible faith in their perceptions of the world around them and the people with whom people communicate, yet all these predictions rely on them. It's normal for you to find people who act in this way, somehow too confident in their abilities at the same time, but only in their abilities that promote negative self-consciousness. Like many of the styles on this list, the mind reader has an incredibly low amount of self-esteem, and so seeks other people's approval and encouragement by stating their negative views of themselves as a fact, or at least as contrary to be. Unlike some of the more hyperbolic forms, like the labeler, their cynical view of the world is not imposed on others by the mind reader. The cynical labeler will return to offending others to justify their own failures or mistakes; the reader in mind simply assumes that people speak about them poorly. Often this "mind-reading" has very little to do with their assessment of the people there. In reality, they frequently find themselves celebrating individuals that they expect think poorly about. We consider all other negative treatment as benefits, as if they are serving an eternal criminal sentence in a past life for their actions. This kind of low self-esteem most often stems from a home life of neglect, or even violence, often mental and emotional— although in most abusive homes, physical and verbal abuse is not often found without one another. Therefore, those who suffer from this kind of thought pit may potentially be best suited for professional help, like counseling, in most serious cases at least. Finding someone licensed to help them get through whatever depression they might have can sometimes be the strongest, or only, the person's road to breaking free from that self-loathing filled loop. We still find it difficult to see the bright side of life, at least for themselves, and really struggle to think of themselves as the norm in the sense that they are "good enough." Whether that means pretty enough, clever enough or tough enough, the mind reader frequently views themselves as exceedingly inferior to their friends and even strangers, about whom they often don't know. We presume the worst of themselves and often take on the best of others. We usually know this way of thinking is wrong, not to mention dangerous, but we lack the confidence and courage to believe enough in themselves to do anything about it. Some of them believe they are always going to be compared to their superiors, and to everyone around them. Whatever influenced them earlier in their lives to make them believe they are terrible people, or just people who will never be deserving of their achievements, accomplishments, or whatever they do some people may find important, or worthy of praise, they believe the influence from others will always be with them, now a part of them resolved never to leave. For some people, it really never does — they turn their trauma as part of their coping mechanism, and drown in cynical pessimism their frustration and worries, thinking they will never improve and life will never get better to them. The best medicine for people who, as I said, are suffering from this kind of thought pit is counseling, which is preferably done beforehand with a support system. Sometimes people who feel that way, who believe they're being manipulated and disliked by everyone around them, need to learn to trust people again before they can erase their critical thinking process. Treatment is typically an excellent way to build up the ability to forgive yourself and trust people around you again. You are not despised for people who feel they may come under the "mind reader" category. You are plenty, and always will be enough.

- Mental filter— a more general description of many different types of people suffering from many different types of thought loops, those with a perceptual barrier or, more simply, a toxic filter, does not automatically perceive the world in a distorted or deluded way. Unlike the mind reader kind, people don't think wrong things about the negative filter. Despite knowing the facts of their situation they don't believe the worst of things and people. Rather, those with a pessimistic filter almost entirely ignore positive aspects of things, or their condition, depending on the severity of their question. People also focus solely on the negative sides of an issue, concentrating on what makes them feel depressed, irritated, alone, frustrated or otherwise placing them in a poor mind frame. This can be for any reason — sometimes, as with many of the other forms, it is a result of negligence in the person's past. Sometimes the former protector of the victim had that same pattern of dwelling only on the negative, and as an infant, the person simply followed suit, as a child does. Sometimes the habit grows clearly on its own, sometimes when the individual has an attitude of contrary. What I mean is that often when a person deliberately puts on a negative attitude that was not explicitly or at least partially caused in the past by their surroundings, the attitude is mostly embraced in the first place because the person in question is mostly irritated. We are hell-bent on being isolated from the mainstream, and thus pursue a much more cynical world view. You might believe you're deluding yourself into thinking the world is better than it actually is when you reflect on the positive side of a situation. It creates almost a kind of fallacy because, then, the person in question turns to the opposite extreme and adopts such a pessimistic perspective that they are themselves deluded into thinking the universe is worse than it really is. This edgy way of looking at the world is normal and gradually evolves into a process of which the individual is often not even really conscious. So, the habit of pessimism chips away at the individual day after day as they become a cynic, unable to form positive thoughts and eventually become a melodramatic shell of their previous self. That's not always the case, of course, for people who look at the world this way. Occasionally, it can evolve from a fear of illusion. People who develop behaviors like this often believe that they are being fooled in some way by being positive. This delusion grows until the individual becomes pathologically pessimistic to the point that, again, they actually follow the opposite side of the spectrum, being deluded into the belief that something bad will happen to optimistic people, and that this occurrence will break their hope and leave them shattered. Apparently the truth is quite the reverse. Those who are more cynical are more likely to be negatively impacted by traumatic or even traumatizing incidents over the long term. On the opposite, those with a more hopeful, confident outlook on life are more likely to be affected in the short term, but because of their positive attitude — ensuring, of course, that this positive attitude remains intact and relatively unchanged after that incident— they will recover quickly and recover further, whilst their negative equivalents seem more to keep on to stuff for an event For example, this can cause a lot of trouble for pessimists, because they are often disillusioned to think they have the upper hand. It comes from the misunderstanding between pessimism and rationality, which later chapters will go into more detail. Pessimism derives from the anticipation of the worse, while optimism has no hope. That disparity plays a central role in how pessimists respond to issues. The best way to "treat" this kind of mind loop is to make sure they stay on the positive side of things as much as possible. Those with a pessimistic outlook on their life often don't understand that things aren't always bad and that being positive doesn't matter. Furthermore, because people with this kind of buffer realize that their condition does not improve if they become more constructive — even if their situation gets improved with this adjustment in perception — they are often far more likely to continue to be more optimistic in the long run.

CHAPTER 4

ESCAPING THE THINKING SINKHOLE, SANDPIT, AND COMMON TRAP

The number of ways in which you believe you can 'go wrong' is enormous and multiple. Perhaps there are too many ways you can go wrong with your thinking, it's about time we discuss the many directions you can change your steps, and go right with your thought instead. So don't worry, it's easy as long as you're reliable.

If working with something of your own making, consistency is the key. If you aren't pushed into something, you need to develop your own power. Unfortunately, the momentary burst of passion and excitement doesn't last forever, especially for someone who doesn't consider themselves to be very exciting people. Nonetheless, you have to replace slow and steady determination with that excitable action and passion. Being diligent in your actions in life also contributes to the satisfaction of the tests. As a wise man once said: "Ambition is the path to greatness. Persistence is the vehicle which you arrive there in." Now that we've been over the different kinds of thought traps that are most common in today's world in more depth, it's important to understand how best to get out of those traps.

Although yes, I've explained some of the more specific things about some of the various pitfalls, as you come to terms with your thought loop, here are some of the more common choices for you.

- Separating your thoughts from reality— as I briefly mentioned in the previous chapter, there really is a huge difference between pessimism and optimism. While yeah, clearly pessimism is to look at things in a negative way and optimism is to look at the beginning reality with both its ups and downs, there's a bit more to it. Pessimism, for one thing, draws all its assumptions from looking at things in a negative light. This draws its conclusions from negative assumptions about the environment and the interactions within it. Meanwhile, there is really nothing reality has to draw conclusions from on its own. Ideally, a realist makes no assumptions other than observations and conclusions that could have been drawn without using human error or partiality. Realism, in a perfect example, uses only factual information and the objective evidence truth to answer questions on that reality. Of reality it is impossible to completely eradicate any human error or prejudice, but preferably, when making an assessment, a realist tries their best to remove any previously existing prejudices. Many people who struggle with thought loops suffer the most because their beliefs and facts are so distant. The disconnection could have resulted from many different places, from abuse in the past to childhood deprivation to a variety of many different things that might have happened in the person's past, but if you're someone struggling to get out of a thought bind and want to attempt to reconcile the truth of your world and your experiences in it, ask yourself some of the following questions when you start" By presenting facts and information that anyone who has observed or engaged in the incident will agree unequivocally without reservation or inference," What do I think?" Analyzing the cognitive process of reasoning, what you're telling yourself, dissecting your feelings so that you can actually tell the difference between the reality of a situation and the conclusions you make based on your past experiences or prejudices that you had before you were put in the scenario," How do I feel?" Analyze your emotions and the impact your thoughts have on your emotional state, learn to distinguish your thoughts from your feelings so that you don't misinterpret them, so that you can make more rational decisions based on unreliable information that you believe is real, but don't know is true, and' How am I coping with that?" Analyze your coping mechanisms to make sure that you are as healthy as possible as you cope with it. Your coping mechanisms may include removing yourself from others so as not to misrepresent your view of the encounter or case, taking deep breaths and relaxing yourself emotionally so that your feelings become more manageable as a result, and relying on your support system to only provide you with knowledge that is impartial and trustworthy, rather than further indulging in the thought pit that induces you It's also important to examine and consider how you actually react to different circumstances as you talk about how you cope with a scenario. Before you even begin to make mistakes and collapse, knowing yourself properly and how you react to things can be a huge stepping stone for you, in terms of helping to better control your potentially dangerous urges.

- Identify your thinking trap— What could be the most important step toward managing your emotions and feeling more positively is to understand why you think the way you do negatively. In other words, one of your first and most critical moves must be to figure out which of the thought loops you associate with most. The method will take a long time before you can definitely say which of the mental loops you consider to be the one you suffer most from, but a simple way to reach the most accurate conclusion is to write down your thoughts as you have them while coping with a specific tension or emotionally strenuous circumstances. When you can better understand which of your thought processes is the most regular and pervasive to you— or, in most instances, which spiral is the most troublesome in your life— you will equate the thought process to the thinking traps mentioned in previous chapters, and see which one you most associate with. Consider where you came from, as well. If you can understand what made you feel pessimistic in the specific way you do in your past, if anything, you will better understand how those negative experiences as a youth or in your childhood would have consequences in your adulthood and correspond with your particular thought pit. Of example, someone who grew up in a particularly competitive or otherwise cutthroat household where you were forced to achieve and excel, such characteristics may come back in the form of strict pragmatism in your adult life, which could manifest negatively in the form of an attitude of "black and white thinking." Note that no two people are exactly the same, so it's highly unlikely you'll encounter a thought pit the same way other people do. A person who has a particular affinity to a negative way of thinking may not fit the typical trend for most people who share the particular trap of thought. This does not make any particular person who shares a thought trap with that thinking trap less or more true in their thinking trap or in their battle with it.

- Challenge your thinking trap— That seems a little too simple to many people, but it's incredibly important to criticize whatever thought-provoking pit you believe you fail the most or have the most trouble fighting your life. While this is somewhat simple, the most important thing about overcoming the thought patterns is remaining committed to fighting them. When asked about thought pits, something many people trip about is that perhaps the most enticing sin known to man is sloth, to be idle. Why would you make an effort to battle something when some of you are so insistent that you can never really get rid of it, no matter what? When part of you know deep down that you're never going to be left with the negative part, what's the point of even trying first? Those are exactly the kinds of ideas you need to know how to isolate yourself from reality before you can start fighting your mental pit. One of the best ways of fighting the pit of thought is simply working in the opposite direction. For starters, if you're a sort of "mind reader," someone who often believes that everybody you've met with dislikes you, in order to fuel your self-loathing, battle the pattern in your thinking by continuously casting doubt on it. Although this may sound counter-intuitive, and it is important to try to invalidate certain negative thoughts as soon as they appear in your head for many of the other forms. This way, doubting certain feelings will become second nature after long enough, just as much as the conclusions were in the first place. Once it becomes so much easier to cast doubt on those feelings because they surface in your head, the next step would be to struggle against the pessimistic perception and to argue. Sometimes, casting doubt is just not enough if the person suffers badly enough from that sort of thinking. If this is the case, and no matter the pit of thinking, battling and struggling against the negative thoughts as much as possible is crucial, moving in the opposite direction to undermine those thoughts. Here are some other things to do while battling the traps in thinking;

- Examination: Take a sharper eye to the bad things you think. The more pessimistic the thinking that emerges in your mind, the more attention that should come under it. The aim here is to make it more stressful on you mentally to have a negative thought than to have a positive one, while people who have such thoughts will just let them pass as natural quite always. The aim is to make the connection between mental analysis and getting such negative thoughts in the first place, so that having those thoughts becomes more hassle than its worth, and the thinking becomes less and less regular.

- Scrutinizing your double-standard: Tell yourself if you'd say the things you do about yourself about others who are close to you. Understand that you and your worth's negative thoughts are anomalous and damaging to yourself and your mental state. Contrast yourself to others in a way that would make you more empathic with yourself, rather than criticizing yourself aggressively out of habit. This approach is made primarily for those who struggle most from a thought pit that requires very harsh self-criticism, such as the thinker "black and white" or the sort of "mind reader" Understanding to distinguish the feelings you have about yourself from reality will allow you to be able to empathize with yourself in the future and become just a little bit more naive to yourself.

- Surveying peers and equals— this form works well particularly for the sort of thought trap "should have, could have, would have." Wherever you have an unwelcome question about whether or not your thoughts and actions are good enough for you, this method involves observing. So, after the idea has been noticed, go around to those you know don't have your issues and remind them what you're having trouble with. For example, if someone has problems with a child or a particular type of job assignment, they may say "good parents / better workers can't have that kind of problem for themselves! I'm not a good worker / parent because I have this problem. "But, it's very often the reverse is entirely true. Usually, whether you question someone who you see as the epitome of what you're trying to be, or like you're failing relative to what they actually think of your case, or how they're really stacking up next to you, you're likely to be surprised by the results— because more often than not, you're the one who's deluded into thinking you're not given a chance against others, or pale in comparison. Understand that almost everybody is going through the same very same challenges. Everyone is different but most people can interact through their experiences. Keep this in mind when you have a feeling that feels like "I'm not as nice as this person or that person," because, like you, it's highly likely that they are the ones who are struggling. You have a lot more in common with your colleagues than you actually would think.

- Conduct your own experiment— we also think of those negative thoughts as a rule of law. We don't consider the possibility that these ideas we've got are impossible. So, try it for yourself next time you're having a string of thoughts around the same subject. Of example, many people have recurring fear that their friends are only really dealing out sympathy on them, or that they feel bad of them. We don't feel like they really know about those friends. Now, they're checking those ideas and texting as many mates as they can to try and make arrangements. Since they were presumably of the opinion that most, if not all, of the friends would refuse the invitation or make an excuse not to follow up, they would definitely be pleasantly surprised when more of the friends accepted the extended invitation than they expected.

Coming out of a pit of thought is in and of itself a daunting task. It certainly isn't unlikely, however. Not for you, or anybody else. Make sure that you are really linking your problems back to you when discussing the thought traps. Sometimes when we don't seem to be able to deal with our challenges or worries of our life, we dissociate ourselves from them and relate these questions instead to a fictional "someone else." In some cases this can help a lot , particularly when you need to make sure your viewpoint is accurate or you need a second opinion. Still, however, we find this is not the case when we need to re-ground ourselves and own up to our own problems. This coping mechanism will quickly turn into a cowardly crutch that lets us comfortably withdraw from our problems. And, when you sit down and try to find a way out of your thought loops, remember that even if you're not alone, nobody can better understand the problems than you can. You must be the one who determines what you, as a human, need. The qualities you are learning by taking a closer look at yourself will most likely come into play and support you later.

CHAPTER 5

HOW THESE THOUGHTS COME TO BE

We get so caught up about what, by nature, these mental loops and unhealthy ideas are, and how to get out of them, but we hardly think deeper about them— where do these thoughts really come from, to continue with? How can such an abnormal pattern of thoughts and actions persist in a person for so long while remaining completely unchecked, even until it is on an extreme level?

In reality, that answer can lie in how we raise our babies. Let me explain a little more: while many people know that one of the many topics you just "just don't speak" to others is how to raise a child "properly." While there is certainly huge debate surrounding this topic, and while for a very good reason it is such a touchy topic, there is something to be said about, maybe, how profoundly awkward this topic makes many of us feel to be debating.

It's hard to raise a child— one of the few things that are universally agreed upon as being a mom. Not only is it complicated, but there is no real solid clear way of raising a child the right way. It is ridiculous to even argue that there is a right way at all, to many. Yet, there are many ways the majority believes that there are poor ways to raise a child. One of those is allowing a parent's bias to negatively impact the infant.

To put it more simply, my mother is working towards a condition with her children where her faults are lacking — she wanted to raise children who knew what she was doing wrong, her shortcomings and benefited from them. Most parents think this way, trying to improve the lives of their kids by somehow encouraging them to both follow in their footsteps and avoid them altogether. "Take like I mean, not like I do," to be more succinct. That is to say, where many parents "go wrong," by the expectations of many other parents, is when they encourage their own vices to take root in their children.

A lot of kids are born in a very competitive environment, for example. Not only can this be anomalous with a certain kind of discipline, it can also be disruptive and even risky to the infant. Kids sometimes fail to understand the meaning behind something forced on them by a parent— young children, often, understand only the fact and the action. Children don't really know or even understand the reason an adult views them in a certain manner, children just remember the way they've been handled and on that basis make assumptions about themselves, others and the world as a whole. As such, the decisions they make affect the way they mature and act as children, and later in their life as adults. Therefore, if they draw an inference about them that is negative depending on how they were handled at school, and how the atmosphere, the community, of their childhood, are the bad patterns that originate in that child's fault indeed entirely? If that is what happens to that boy, does even matter the reason behind that upbringing? The answer to this question, in my personal experience, is "no," but that's up for debate.

Therefore, we have to wonder now, is a dysfunctional girl unstable only because of her upbringing? Is it just and always the guardian's fault that a child is the way they are? Yet, perhaps more critically, why are children making such dangerous decisions, and why are they later creating what we now perceive as chains of thinking and toxic behavior?

To go back to that scenario, let's presume you have a friend named Isaac, who was born his entire life in a very competitive environment for example. His home life was not only competitive-it was nothing short of cutthroat. He was made to feel devalued and insignificant because he struggled to excel and adhere to his parents ' expectations. Your friend Elijah was very rarely allowed to run around and play outdoors, because of such a strong insistence on performance in all fields. We weren't allowed to hang out with their peers, play games, or have a lot of what we'd deem a normal childhood or a lot of a childhood.

So, take a step back and think for a moment about that example: how do you think this kind of atmosphere would impact your friend in the long run of their lives? How would that childhood—or lack of it — influence their adulthood, and how they functioned socially after that sort of education?

Jumping back into the fray of that case, your friend Elijah has now grown into something of an introvert, even though he tries hard to connect with his peers and make friends. It just doesn't seem to work out for him and he doesn't seem to realize why. He gets upset that he doesn't seem to be able to get in touch with people he wants to get along with and make plans with. On another note, Elijah struggled with recognition and rivalry much in his adulthood. He has a significant competitive streak, one that comes mostly from his parents and his earlier years. Furthermore, this competitive streak will gradually grow from a friendly but tough attitude to someone who really can't lose to someone else physically. If he fails everything he tries at — that is, everything— Elijah obviously gets upset and feels dejected. Even the most insignificant of defeats, he takes against him as a personal slight and because of that, he feels betrayed by the people around him. On top of that, he thrives off of support from any direction that comes to him, especially people he looks up to and loves. The undying need for that affirmation is more or less what pushes him to be productive, though he acknowledges that for him and the peers this way of thinking is incredibly unhealthy. While he needs to be stronger and have a greater self-esteem, he is bound to his success by his self-worth. He acknowledges that this isn't safe at all, but he doesn't seem to be able to find any other way to measure his personal worth. Neither does his ambitious career help — it just brings him further and further down to the belief that all he does is to appease a higher authority figure. He goes further and further down the rabbit hole every time he indulges those desires. He says that he wants to stop feeling this way, because he gets little or no pleasure from it, even if he helps someone. The surge of gratification that he gets to satisfy someone is a temporary sensation, which will quickly be replaced by the desire for more, bigger, greater. Often because of his reckless actions he drives himself far too hard and experiences physical consequences.

If any of that sounds like either you or someone you know, you or a loved one are likely to suffer from an incredibly common form of thought, one that has arisen more and more over the past decade or so. Most parents follow a sort of a hybrid between a parent of a helicopter and a parent of the Drill Sergeant Type: a kind of parent who watches over their child but only in the way a teacher supervises their pupil. This kind of parent takes the technique of erasing your child's flaws to a whole new, extreme level. In trying to teach and encourage their child to be the best and stronger versions of their parents, they have given their child a whole new set of issues and challenges which they will have to deal with later in life. When all you know about learning and graduation in your childhood and you know that achieving high grades and studying a lot makes your father or guardian happy and proud, you quickly learn how to put these two things together. If you're only used to feeling like a good child when you're academically successful, what hope do you really have of growing up into a well-rounded adult? Absolutely, none. Your chances of growing up and being able to accept your failures and your faults without getting upset with yourself and others is none the slim. Of course, the blame for that rests with the parent who — sometimes unintentionally, but nevertheless — instilled in you as a young child that it is to be successful for them to be worth someone as an individual. That kind of philosophy translates well into their schooling, as most forms of education follow a similar model of thought. The very same children who lived their lives in fear of being unproductive and thus unloved thrived in that system of education. The relationship between them and their education only further strengthened the connection between their importance and their academic achievements. In a way, we have to draw the line and ask ourselves whether or not this success is really worth it in our children, from both a realistic and a spiritual perspective.

On the one side, sometimes quickly burn out those kids who are pushed so hard all their lives. Children are often viewed as special cases, children who surpass any of their more "normal peers." Because of this special treatment, many of these kids have the idea in their heads that they are not just superior in some inherent sense than those peers, but they are also indoctrinated into believing that this distinction between them and the rest of the world is going to exist for ever. As they get older, when this theory comes crashing down around them, it can have terrible effects on their emotional health and performance as well. Coming at it even from the viewpoint of someone who wants to raise a kid who is educated and successful above all else, wouldn't it be much better— both for the parent and the child in question — to raise a child who can maintain himself and take good care of his health, both physically and emotionally? It has been proven time and time again that people who learn how to manage themselves job-wise and in all other areas of their lives are shown to be more competitive across all fields and at the same time more likely to be successful and happy, a task that becomes even harder to achieve when you are so focused on your career that you completely disregard pleasure. Therefore, also with the selfish goals of this kind of parent, it works in both their favor and the youth's favor to raise a child who is well-rounded enough to take care of himself and understand how to manage the importance of his satisfaction and how much he needs, and also to understand the importance of self-gratification rather than being out of the admiration of figures of authority,

On the other hand, we will approach parenting the child from the viewpoint of a caring and compassionate parent who knows that joy actually fulfills a child more than being successful, and that this satisfaction translates into their adult lives even better than mere success, in particular the sense of individuality that so often escapes us as we get. The reason that some kids get about the feeling is that it comes from the fact that as kids they are far above their peers. We may be in elementary school and reading at a high school level, or even reading at college level. The further you go into life, though, while embracing your talent as inevitable and doing nothing to improve it further, the more your peers — many of whom are learning and constantly improving their skills to keep up with everyone else— catch up with you. Everyone reads at high school or college level soon enough and you are now an ordinary example of a reader. You avoid being the poster child of academic success and slip off the top rank. This sense of mediocrity drives for children a curious change in self-perception: what used to be a child with a complex of dominance is now a child with a complex of rather extreme inferiority. The two contrary circumstances don't always balance out, and sometimes they just tend to coexist within this person who somehow wants to be flawless and all right away as they pick it up, and also thinks dangerously poorly of themselves. The odd dichotomy of grandeur and self-loathing also fits together to form some of the chains of thinking that we often see and explored in previous chapters.

Of course, there are other ways in which the manner a father treats his offspring will strongly influence the way children act when they grow up and become an independent adult. Sometimes you see parents who are behaving in a way that is totally contradictory to that stern and rigid parent, a parent who is not only constantly acting on their child, but is also constantly acting to protect their child from any danger that comes their way. While this protective behavior may come in handy when the child is simply just a survivor and/or in danger, if it takes the form of not only that particular kind of circumstance, but also situations where the child is the target of abuse, or otherwise to blame for the penalty that they would get without the intervention of the parents. Refusing to allow your kid to view the world in a way that is realistic enough to let them learn from their mistakes essentially opens up a world of opportunities for the kind of abuse that may eventually become their newest habit. Of example, many kids who are let off the hook of things they actually did wrong when their parents interfered, now have the idea in their minds that they can get away with much more than they had originally thought, without penalty, since their parent or guardian originally allowed them to. Of example, parental involvement can counteract that, but the more a child has that connection made and unregulated in their head, the easier the pattern is to undo. This allows the child to behave entirely as they wish with little to no consequence on their conduct. We become devious and cynical, and in some situations can even become abusive. Nonetheless, this is most certainly not the child's fault, not completely at least — no, in this situation, to blame we will look to the adult, who permitted their child to do whatever they wished with their actions without repercussions. The adult who unwittingly gives their child a complex of gods, encouraging them to wreak havoc if they so wish because they know for a fact that nothing is going to happen to them, regardless of what they do or do. This form of parenting will severely damage the child when he or she becomes an adult, both in the sense of his or her social ability and the real productivity. If you feel like whatever you do, your decisions are either overlooked or simply forgotten, you lose a sense of moral responsibility that most other people cultivate and mature as they age. Not only that, but this right being lost can have serious long-term effects of a child's life. Not only can they easily turn themselves into a spiteful person capable of great malicious acts, but they can also transform themselves into an individual who is not at all usable as we see it. Although they seem to function properly, they struggle to have much of the inherent knowledge that "average" children do about social groups. Interestingly, when a parent attempts to excessively socialize their child by encouraging them to do basically whatever they want, they not only set them up for disappointment, but at the same time set them on the road to being socially inept, insecure autistic children unable to communicate and connect with people who would normally be their natural peers.

It's strange how all of this goes back to how greedy a parent can be with his kids. Though there are the "true" parents, of course, as we deem them, who would basically do anything to make their child happy while retaining a social hierarchy and a sense of responsibility for them. Although there are many distinct and often contrasting opinions of what constitutes a perfect parent, most people agree that it is better for most children to have a caring and strict family. Such guardians aren't so stern that they might be seen as a traditional parent of "Drill Sergeant," or so loose and doting that they might be called parents of the helicopter, but they usually find their room somewhere in the middle of those two extremes. Those parents are much more likely to be able to make "healthy" and "natural" kids who work just fine and are more than able to thrive within the rest of our society without any other intervening influences. Instead, completely on the other side of that continuum, you have what we find to be "evil" parents, who lack the patience or desire to allow themselves treat their children as individuals rather than objects for their amusement or as trophy cases for their pride. How we find imperfect parents as perfect parents appears in many different forms, from too loose to not lax enough. It should be noted that in such situations this kind of bad parenting creates "bad babies," but— a bit like we think of bad owners, not bad pets— the child's misery almost always lies with the adult, who has neglected their "work" as a parent to keep their child healthy and as comfortable as practicable, despite the environment.

There are many avenues to go wrong, of course, and almost all of them are controllable stuff, though some of them are not. There are certain things we can just never expect to control in our lives. There are things we can actively try to avoid, to swerve on our life's road to avoid crossing paths with some unsightly occurrence, but sometimes it just can't help. Things like that happen, and it's easier to be ready for it than to be willing to give up ship if you hit a bump on the track. In reality, the feeling takes us to the other major factor in negative thinking— not just how we are treated in our homes as children, but the atmosphere in which we communicate with our peers. This is in part in reference to the public education system, although it might also be taken to refer to the much wider scale of today's ever-changing society.

Simply put, the sort of environment that develops in generation after generation as preteens and young adults change and changes as different generations pass across life stages. From the laxer and more carefree world of children in the 80s and

90s, or what is referred to as "Gen X"— which is perhaps the coolest name imaginable for a bunch of 30-somethings— to the more modern social atmosphere that has welcomed children, particularly in the US, with more stressful news than ever before. As the line between fear mongering and simple alert is increasingly blurred, the way children respond and take in details theoretically often changes when their sensitization increases. Although Gen Y, or "millennials," which is the group that is now mostly in their twenties, has been relatively normal with this rapidly changing culture, even psychologists who have conducted studies of young people's mental states agree that the levels of stress, depression, and anxiety are growing year after year, now at the equivalent of an institutionalized patient in the sixties. With that in mind, we now look to the generation that is actually in high school and higher education, Generation Z. Gen Z, as we know it, is undoubtedly the most stressed out, sleep deprived, nervous generation ever, and the one that follows after it is likely to continue the pattern. So; what went wrong in so many lives to make this such a drastic change, such an unprecedented plunge in our last frontier mental state— our student?

The answer comes directly from the public education system as many would expect. With a relatively new drive to be popular, more kids are throwing themselves into a program that gets a little tougher every year, working hard to join extracurricular activities that take up even more of their time just to get into the college they think will help them reach that goal, to be able to live a happy and fulfilling life. Most people have the idea hammered into them that if they work hard enough they're never going to suffer as much in life as those who don't work as hard. This is simply not true, since most students learn very quickly. In reality, the opposite is true— those students who drive themselves are often the ones who end up hurting more when they go on to college, when they are piled up with even more education and are now faced with the burdens of life without parental supervision or the warmth of their loved ones right in front of them. Rather, they have to face the world entirely alone now; at least, that's how it looks and how it feels to many students today.

Once you start feeling trapped, you feel isolated. Some students, especially college students who now have substantially less interaction with their loved ones than they did while living at home, report feeling much more lonely. Negative thinking goes along with that isolation. Feeling isolated from your loved ones and your mates, and experiencing immense pressure to succeed without seeing the true value of pursuing a fulfilling career in life, most graduates, even those who have been the most successful and motivated of their peers earlier in life, will plunge into a frightening spiral of self-doubt and hatred. That can spiral out of control very easily and become a challenge that may not be fully recognized by those students, or know how to fix if they do.

As it happens, this kind of reasoning has been more or less normalized with Gen Z in particular. Whether it's for college or high school students, this way of thinking so little of yourself that it has driven up the tension even more, as an odd circular and inadequate way to cope with that stress spread like wildfire — especially with the help of a still relatively new tool for teens, social media, throughout culture. The social media can be a big boost in spreading the gospel of other students connected to young people who otherwise feel like they have no one to communicate with or reach out to. While social media is most certainly something of a saving grace, it can also be a crutch for many people, particularly those students who are especially susceptible to coercion and manipulation when their other alternative is to be all alone. Yet frankly, not everybody on social media is a good influence or someone whose strategies work for everyone, or anyone else. While that much is clear, it can still be a psychologically and emotionally challenge for students to determine whether to be alone or to feel connected within a society that is, at its heart, toxic to all involved parties.

How can anyone ever expect to get stronger with the kind of mentality that becomes the hidden enemy for many young people being normalized? Actually things aren't as grim as they might seem. In fact, while there are a large number of young people, especially those in Generation Z, who think this way, who are self-deprecating for the sake of using humor as a sort of coping mechanism, there is another, even more recent surge in the actions of young people and teens that takes advantage of the impact well-known social media influencers have on each other and on their viewers. That way of thinking critically and being socially "happy"-offers young people a path and social affirmation to join such social media influencers and reach out and genuinely seek support. If, previously, the notion of suffering in silence for the dark beauty was alluring, and was the only style that those influencers promoted and supported, today those very same public figures are at the forefront of the discussion about how we cope with our pressures, both the older and younger generations in the modern world. Most importantly, tension builds in crowds with social media influencers, and many of them with a purer heart feel the need to fix the friction to resolve the very real mental health crisis we have in classrooms that affect children and teenagers much more easily than in the past generations. Today, the debate is not only conducted on social media by younger people, but is also taken into account by older people, merely because that dangerous situation becomes too noisy, too clear, to be overlooked or pushed aside any longer. The mental health of youth and that youth's negative thinking is so strong and unhealthy now, and we must all come together as a society and as a world to make a concerted effort to help those in great need. Whether they are our babies, the friends of our children or the peers we fear are in danger of succumbing to their own terrible thoughts, we who serve the rest of the world are, in some sense, personally responsible for those who cannot mentally care for themselves for whatever purpose. People, parents, elders, mates, colleagues, and superiors, must step up and care for each other, and protect and support those who don't know how to help themselves — such as the rule of any environment, no matter how cutthroat; everyone within the community needs each other, and they all benefit from each other's abilities and strengthen each other in their shortcomings.

So, as we go forward with that information, I hope it gives you a little insight on what sorts of things young people, and all people around the world, are experiencing within their own minds. Read it so that you can learn how to help those around you, those you love and those you care for, if you're not just doing this to support yourself. For help other victims of something you do not need to be a victim of something. It is the camaraderie that comes with facing the world in all its terrors that brings people together and maintains a relationship in which all sides recognize their obligations and shield each other from other things, or from themselves. Whether it's simply talking to that person or consciously ensuring they get the support they might need, do your part to make sure people around you are taken care of. Denying treatment to others, and the knowledge that they are cherished is also cruelly revoking the person's meaning of life.

CHAPTER 6

HANGING IN THE BALANCE

When, in some way or another, you are simply someone who indulges in theory a lot, you have undoubtedly pondered the true importance of keeping things relatively orderly. As I said in this book before, voicing the balance you want in your life is so incredibly important. Leaning toward an extreme one way or another will eventually only lead to more frustration of feeling unfulfilled. That's also why a lot of people say you might have too much, really. It's not hard to overwhelm anything you like or love, or feel like you need. While this applies to binge-eating, some kind of compulsion, or just the desire to be satisfied by getting too far into something, an obsession or a passion or something completely different, the risk of too much or too little is actually far larger than you think.

Also, we have no idea of the risks of either doing too much or too little of something. Normally, when we notice a bad thing that we normally do and want to stop as soon as we can, we quickly try to stop it all at once, like cutting cold turkey when you used to smoke a cigarette a day. It has not only been in the way that it isn't good for you, it has weakened you and your body physically. It has the ability to send your body and mind into something like a panic state, too disturbed by your conflicting actions to do anything but keep watching with abject horror as you swing back and forth from top to bottom, from left to right, to bottom, from extreme to extreme to extreme, with no real idea of your advancement. We would like to do that because it feels good. When we can tell we left quicker and more profoundly than our colleagues we feel so much more accomplished. Everything can quickly and easily transform into a peer-to-peer rivalry, even stuff that should be to our very own gain. Yet, that's not the way it should be. If you want to stop doing something, make sure you can keep track of your progress— whether that includes tracking stuff you do to get rid of your toxic and destructive thought habits, or joining a group online or in person with someone like you who can help and support you when you need to, it doesn't matter in what medium you consider a support system, but it's always nice. Vocalizing your success and throwing yourself out when you want to leave something, is also really good. It not only eliminates the temptation to separate yourself from anyone you care about, but it also persuades you to follow up on the promises you may have made to the camera and posted online in a blur of the moment, fire of passion. That way, take your competitive spirit and use it to your benefit. Challenge yourself regularly, to make sure you don't take any prisoners. Having a consistent and aggressive attitude about kicking the habit is one of the many keys of effectively breaking a bad habit, other than juggling and knowing you have a good support system. The more you are able to detach the hatred you have for yourself, and pin it on that bad habit instead, the happier you'll be in the long run.

Of course, the risks that may happen when you don't take the advice and choose to swing back and forth from one extreme side of something to another must be taken into consideration. Take water, for example,— a need to be alive, an absolute necessity if you want to be safe or usable. Water is incredibly healthy, it has no calories, it refreshes you, it can help with weight loss and it has many other small yet proven benefits to wellness. Therefore, somebody who is trying to get more hydrated will plunge head-first into their latest obsession on drinking more water. While this does not cause a lot of problems in and of itself, it can evolve to be something that causes considerable damage to your life.

For course everyone knows the risks of not getting enough water to drink. Your mouth begins to feel gritty when you're dehydrated, so you start feeling sick. You lose the sharp focus that you might have had when you were hydrated, and you become far less efficient all around you than you would be if you were properly hydrated earlier that day. When that hydration occurs, the distinction between what is actually exhausted and what entails being rushed to the hospital and getting to have an

IV in your arm can be hard to draw. If you become very dehydrated, your condition can deteriorate rapidly and very quickly, even without you knowing. This is what happens to most people who are suffering from a sunstroke— they simply don't know when to find, then they are now approaching the point where they have to drink water if they don't want to unexpectedly become weak. Because they don't actually know how to identify these signals, many of those who suffer from sunstroke are victims of that sort of thing and are blamed for it. We live with the knowledge that we risk their safety and perhaps even their life by stubbornly following someone's advice.

On the flip side of that, a lot of people compulsively drink water. This may be trying to get rid of their oral fixation, sometimes even quitting smoking, or it may just be because that person happens to be on a new fixation with some form of technique of wellness or weight loss. While water is a good way to lose weight and decrease appetite, people who drink tons of it often don't get the rewarding benefits they may want. As I said, the results are gradual and rather mild, if not balanced by that person's workout and a shift in eating habits. At any point, a lot of people only enjoy drinking water for their mental and physical pleasure. Although in its own practice, just for its own sake, that's good, some people go too far with that. Obsessive people who may be hell-bound to their current obsession may over-hydrate, which is as dangerous as being dangerously dehydrated. When you drink an excessive amount of water in a relatively short time frame, a time frame comparable to the amount of water you ingest, the sodium level in your blood will plummet and can have extremely harmful and even lethal consequences on your system. The main cause of death from drinking too much water is just that, the disease of having incredibly low sodium in your blood, often called "water poisoning." Though it may sound a bit crazy, water poisoning takes a significant number of lives each year. There's also a trend for younger people to drink more water right now, as the dark look of being depraved has fallen from favor and the modern image of good skin and good health has come in instead to replace the aesthetic. This drive could easily sway other young people to put themselves at greater risk for this kind of disease which can be extremely dangerous for them and their safety. And, though you should definitely drink plenty of water every day, of course, there's something to say about doing anything to the full, no matter what it is.

Still, what about things that aren't real, may you ask? Yeah, you may have too much or too little food, too much or too little water, too little or too much sleep, exercise, sex, what do you have. Yet, is there really something to tell about the possibility of overloading? Too much confidence? Feeling too happy?

The reaction to that is, put it simply, absolutely. When we gage what is and what is not too much or too little of something so elusive and intangible as love, confidence, hope, happiness or sorrow, we may say from personal experience within ourselves and with others that, yes, you may have too much or too little of something spiritual.

Also, the scale of events that don't have a physical manifestation of a physical basis is much harder to judge; certain people can actually suffer from depression. In reality, the disorder is heart strings that break down from pressure to heart, allowing the heart itself to crumble in on itself and kill the body from within. While it is a physical reaction to something more abstract, it may be due to intense emotion, namely desperation, the strain to the heart. Typically that would be something like a heartbreak— no pun intended— including breakup from a longtime partner, a loved one's death, or something else just as crippling the human. This sorrow can destroy a person solely in the emotional sense, but it can actually destroy them from that sort of misery in the literal sense of fatality. Likewise, given the context and the correct degree, rage can also have this sort of effect on someone. Any feeling, actually, can have an effect on somebody like this. It's just something that poses a far more real danger to us as humans than we might have known before. Emotions and passion will flame us out, in much calmer terms. For example, those things definitely aren't anything that causes death or equally extreme effects, but they're nothing to ignore the findings. Remember that, the first few months are perfect when dating someone new. You feel so deeply in love, like this guy has to be the perfect match for you, your always and forever. You feel stronger than you have ever been, and you burst to shout out to the universe how much you love them, and they feel exactly the same way. We want to show you all off and you two are joined at the hip. Yet, unexpectedly, and from nowhere, the "spark" just seems to die suddenly. Immediately the two of you are no longer as connected, it feels overwhelming to be around them, you no longer go on spontaneous walks late at night, no more of those fun and friendly nights, and what you used to view as their adorable quirks and eccentricity are now things you can't bear, things that get in the way of your already busy and stressful life. You feel awful, and so they and neither of you have any idea why. You don't think something bad happened to tear you apart from one another in your relationship, but you don't know how to explain this abrupt "death" of what you might have thought was your passion. And, what the fuck did you two do?

The harsh reality is, you weren't even in love from the beginning— you were completely infatuated with your partner nonetheless. Most people would tell you that you fell out of love, but more of the reverse is actually true. To fact, you're beginning the first stage of actually loving someone, which allows you to step out of a relationship's first phase, also called the

"Honeymoon Phase." This process has a lot of dopamine and other reward chemicals swirling around within the brain for pretty much all the time, and it's just those hormones, serotonin and adrenaline and all the rest that make you feel so enthusiastic towards them. You are still not having a genuine connection. And you feel incredibly in love with your ideal self and yourself. When you sound so excited about yourself and your partner's interpretations alike, the subconscious just interprets the emotion as "true love," rather than what it truly is under the rose-colored glasses — infatuation that eventually dies after a few months. The honeymoon period of a relationship lasts from a few months to a year and a half, and after that, you know the sensation of an inevitable drop-off. You no longer feel like you miss them because you don't have a constant stream of hormones running into you anymore. But, now you have the ruts from those chemicals in your head. You have room in your head where those thoughts and hormones will flow through you like they usually do, but their intrusion during the honeymoon phase has made the part of your brain that is interacting with your significant other fried. The brain needs time to recover again and you will feel as though the "spark" between the two of you has totally died up until then. This part of love almost never lasts as long as the other phase which came a few months ago. It depends on the person and the strength of their honeymoon phase and their significant other. Most partners do not make it past that point but those who do are rewarded with a relationship that is often endgame or at least rather long-term and ideally satisfying. After the dead flame period, the "heart" reignites in the form of the next step, and the cycle begins again, revived now that the infatuation has been replaced by a more genuine, stronger, truer passion in the third and final phase of most endgame relationships— the phase in which you really know more about each other, become best friends on top of your relationship, and become unified for good this time.

While that's a tangent, it shows you can potentially have too much love as long as that love comes in chemicals type. If we do them too much we get sick of things that we do. That's why, even though it's a great song, it gets killed when a decent song gets heard way too much on the radio. We dislike it, because how much we hear it against our will is becoming irritating.

Too much, too little of something, too big or too small, the way we teach our kids, the way we grow our kids, the way we live as babies. All these things converge and work to make the current phenomenon of negative thinking what we believe to be. The way to stop is in the hands of the people who made it, and the families that are hurting because of it. It's good if you want to give up on your negative thinking and become happier and healthier. Yet, I don't think you'd want to do that if you'd read this far into a book about breaking just that bad habit. Just remember that, no matter what, you have the ability to do whatever you think is right inside of you. The power is in you, it's always been within you and it'll always be within you. All matters is whether you have any confidence in yourself and the people who love you and value you, or not. Those are the ones you need most, except that you are yourself.

CHAPTER 7

WHAT IT MEANS TO BE POSITIVE

You encountered people who are insufferably happy in your life. Everything just falls off their back and into the puddles that they play in like a kid. We seem so curiously positive and happy-go-lucky; it is almost as though they have never received bad news in their entire lives. Not only is watching them going through life like every day is indescribably bright kind of off-putting, but it could also make you very worried about their mental health. After all, you've probably learned more than just that, under a grin, is often a very lonely, very broken, and very frightened guy. It can be difficult to keep the façade intact but some people manage to do it well and do it for a very long time before the cracks begin to show up. You might say to yourself, maybe this is one of those men. Within their metaphorical armor, they never reveal the chink; they still support but never ask for it in exchange. I could go on and on with this hypothetical person for ever, because they're all known. Yet, you would be right — none really is that optimistic. If they are, it may potentially be as dangerous as having negative thoughts in the normal sense.

Simply put, what I mean by that is you've got to have a balance in all aspects of your life. I've scratched all kinds of people for being just a little too pessimistic, not giving in to all of them, victimizing themselves, and doing numerous other things that feel better at the moment but don't really fix something, but maybe all of those things don't even scratch the surface of what some people do is worse than worrying about themselves and others. As I said in the last essay, going from one extreme to the next just causes mental shock; it throws you into a panic state and leaves you confused about what to do with yourself. To act excessively is something like a purely human trait, in a strange way. It's weird, it's dangerous, and it inevitably ends in disaster, but it's a tendency that we can't all seem to be kicked in.

When you go through your life constantly or almost constantly pushing yourself to be positive and happy, you are focused on killing the reasonable part of yourself which is especially good at pointing out faults and weaknesses in situations. The key of a compromise between being a scathing pessimist and getting the unhealthy feelings that have been brought under the microscope this whole time, and being a scathing optimist— someone who is so hopeful that it's unhealthy and, in many instances, delusional — is being able to step back to examine the flaws in something but remain happy while making adjustments.

Although it seems similarly dangerous, any time you try to detach yourself from your shortcomings, just as long as you take a serious, long look at them in a practical, yet vital way. It harms not only our ego, but it affects our performance as well, as we bind ourselves to feedback and take it as a personal insult. If we feel like one person in our lives hates us— even if they don't really— then that same distrust is about everybody else in our lives, and we flee into the safe space in our own minds, where we can disappear underneath all that negative thinking and victimization until someone is willing to show that they matter enough for us to pull us out of our mental canyon. However, as we consciously decide not to take things personally, the unintentionally hurtful comment will turn into something much better, something more positive than you can use to strengthen yourself rather than having the remark to get you down and add fuel to your negative thinking. Nonetheless, we always like to believe that somehow, one day, we're going to have someone there to save us from just about everything in the world, our knight in shining armor or just a friend or mother to hug us and support us and make us feel like we don't have to do anything, as it's not our fault.

Unfortunately, the truth isn't almost that pretty— you need to be the one and only one to dig yourself out of your emotional canyon. While it may be frightening to do so, we will be our own knight in shining armor. Collectively we have to abandon the idea that someone will come to save you whenever we want, whenever we need them. This sort of thinking is what makes us compliant, submissive, and what helps to keep us in that cage of negative thoughts, which lets us sink ever further into our brains. We're slipping further and further into the trap of not having to take the lead and go forward with our own lives. That's something far closer to the truth sadly.

While nobody ever wants to do something on their own, people who have that kind of negative thinking do it very rarely because they want to. Most don't want to talk like that, but in a way they know it's just like their "programming." Their entire lives, or at least most of their childhood, has been packed with their parents or guardians protecting them and assuring them that whatever mess they do, it is not their fault and it is not their job to clean up for it. No, at the time the burden fell entirely upon them, the parent or guardian who watched over the boy. In fact, caring for oneself is not the child's work, simply because no one else will. We have no idea how to take responsibility for their actions, and they don't know how to take responsibility for doing something wrong in the first place without having people turn against them. However, here's another secret— what you do doesn't initially identify you as a human. The opportunities that you get, the luck you have, don't really rely on you. What is reflective of you, however, is how you react to the cards you have been dealt over the course of your life. If you choose to disregard the weight of what you've done, it shows strongly that you're somebody who hates accountability, somebody who possibly can't handle commitment, and many other things that aren't exactly great to have said about you. Yet, no matter what you've done wrong in the past if you courageously own it, it represents the exact opposite of you. Even though you have done something wrong, sometimes something is simply inexcusable for the task or the work or whatever circumstance it may have happened in, it reflects well on you that you accepted it and at least put forth an honest effort of goodness to better yourself and the condition in which you were positioned. That not only needs the confidence within you to take responsibility, but it also requires a lot of positive — or at least realistic — thinking. As we leave high school as kids to go to whatever college we may have chosen, we always abandon a life built for us all our lives. Whether or not we admit it, whether we like it or not, we really start missing the order. This came from our parents, yes, and back then our least favorite teachers, but it was still order, something that gave us a sense of purpose, and that at the time meant a lot to us. We just loved not knowing exactly what to do. Even getting to follow the instructions throughout the day is soothing. When we leave high school and go off to live alone, we always leave behind our parents and teachers and we have to start building our own foundation. That, can be mortifying in itself. Even though we may be very individualized and autonomous, we as humans naturally pack animals and never like having to be surrounded by people we consider foreign. They just don't work like other animals, flying alone, living alone and working alone in the best way. Even though in today's modern world, learning to live like that could potentially turn out to be better for our mental wellbeing.

The point is all of the negative thoughts aren't toxic. The universe is messy sometimes and bad things happen, it is an important part of the way we all live. It's happened before and it's bound to happen to you and everyone else. You don't have success every day but don't let that either stop you from trying to find the evil in it. In everything that we are there are good things and good people, in everything we do. The planet is working like this. You can be sad— you can have bad days and you will be guided through by the people who love you. You can have those feelings of rage and deep sorrow. You can weep and yell or leap for happiness, but realize that without the other, you can't have one, so know how to have both in your life. If you can learn how to put the balance into practice, you'll have a more fulfilled life, both good and bad.

HOW TO IMPROVE YOUR EMOTIONAL INTELLIGENCE

1. Utilize an assertive style of communicating.

Assertive contact is going a long way in earning respect without being too hostile or defensive. Individuals who are emotionally intelligent know how to communicate their thoughts and desires openly while respecting others.

2. Respond instead of reacting to conflict.

Emotional outbursts and feelings of anger are normal during contrasting instances. The person with an emotional intelligence knows how to remain calm in stressful situations. We do not make impulsive decisions which can lead to even greater problems. We recognize that the aim is a settlement in times of conflict, and we make a conscious decision to concentrate on how their actions and words agree with that.

3. Utilize active listening skills.

Throughout discussions, people with emotional intelligence listen for clarification, rather than just waiting for their turn to speak. Until responding, they ensure they understand what's being said. We even take care of the nonverbal aspects of a discussion. It avoids misunderstandings, allows the listener to respond appropriately and displays respect for the person to whom they talk.

4. Be motivated.

Emotionally intelligent people are self-motivated, and others are inspired by their mindset. We are setting goals and they are resilient to challenges.

5. Practice ways to maintain a positive attitude.

Don't underestimate your attitude's might. A negative attitude will quickly corrupt others if one person permits it. Emotionally smart people have an understanding of the moods of those around them and their behavior is controlled appropriately. We learn what to do to get a good day and a positive outlook. This might involve having a great breakfast or lunch, investing in Morning Prayer or meditation, or keeping meaningful quotations at their office or screen.

6. Practice self-awareness.

People with emotional intelligence are self-conscious and intuitive. They become mindful of their own feelings, and how those around them can be influenced. We also focus on the thoughts and body language of others, and use that information to improve their communication skills.

7. Take critique well.

A significant part of improving your emotional intelligence is being able to take criticism. Instead of becoming upset or angry, people with high EQ take a few minutes to consider where the criticism comes from, how it impacts someone or their own success and how they can resolve any issues constructively.

8. Empathize with others.

Those who are mentally wise learn how to empathize. We recognize that empathy is a quality that shows strength in the heart, not vulnerability. Empathy allows people, on a basic human level, to respond to others. It opens the door to mutual respect and understanding among people with different opinions and different situations.

9. Utilize leadership skills.

Emotionally smart people possess excellent leadership skills. We have high standards, which set an example for others to follow. You have great decision-making and problem-solving capabilities and take initiative. It makes a higher and more efficient level of performance both at work and in life.

10.   Be approachable and sociable.

Those who are socially savvy come off as approachable. They are laughing and showing off a good look. We use appropriate social skills based on their relationship to whoever we are around. We have excellent interpersonal skills, and we know how to communicate plainly, through vocal or nonverbal contact.

To those who understand basic human psychology, many of these abilities may seem best suited. Although high EQ skills can come to inherently empathic people more quickly, they can be learned by anyone. More empathetic people just need to practice becoming more self-conscious and aware of how they communicate with others. By using those measures, you will be well on the way to through your level of emotional intelligence.

HOW TO BOOST SELF CONFIDENCE

1. Stay away from negativity and bring on the positivity

This is the time to evaluate your inner circle in real terms, like friends and family. This is a difficult one, but it's time to consider seriously walking away from those people who put you down and shred your trust.

Be confident, even if you don't see it as yet. Bring some constructive energy into your relationships with others, and hit the running track, ready to launch your next job. Stop focusing on your life's problems, and start focusing on ideas and making positive improvements instead.

2. Change your body language and image

It is here where stance, smile, eye contact and voice come into play slowly. Just the simple act of pulling back your shoulders gives the impression to others that you're a confident person. Not only will laughing make you feel better but it will make others feel more relaxed around you. Imagine a person with a good posture and a smile and you'll imagine someone who's confident in himself.

Look at the person you're referring to, not your shoes— keeping the eye contact indicates confidence. Next, speak slowly. Evidence has shown that those who take the time to speak slowly and clearly feel more faith in themselves and look more positive towards others. The added bonus is that they really will be able to understand what you're doing.

Go the extra mile to style your hair, put on a clean shave, and dress up beautifully. This not only makes you feel better for yourself, but also makes others more likely to view you as positive and self-confident. A great tip: If you buy a new dress, first try wearing it at home to get over any malfunctions in your closet before going out.

3. Don't accept failure and get rid of the negative voices in your head

Never concede. Always embrace default. Everything has a remedy, so why would you want to throw in the towel? Build your new mantra to this. Success through considerable difficulty is a big catalyst for morale.

Low self-confidence is often induced by the constant trail of negative thoughts going through our heads. If you're constantly bashing yourself and thinking that you're not nice enough, aren't pretty enough, aren't clever enough or talented enough, and you're building a prophecy that is self-fulfilling. Within your brain you are what you are teaching, and that's not healthy. The next time you hear the negative in your mind, turn it to a positive affirmation right away and hold it up until it reaches the level of a lift of self-confidence.

4. Be prepared

Know all you need to learn about your industry, career, presentation — whatever's next on the "to win" list. If you're confident and have the skills to help it, your self-confidence will grow.

5. For tough times, when all else fails: Create a great list

Life is full of obstacles and there are times when our self-confidence is hard to keep up. Sit down now and make a list of all the things you're grateful for in your career, and another list of all the accomplishments you're proud to do. When your lists are full, paste them on your fridge door, on your office wall, on your bathroom mirror— somewhere you can easily remember what an amazing life you've had and what a wonderful person you really are. When you find that your self-confidence is dwindling, take a look at those lists and let yourself be encouraged by you all over again.

HOW TO IMPROVE YOUR SELF-ESTEEM

1. Use positive affirmations correctly

Positive statements like "I'll be a great success!" They are extremely popular, but they have one critical problem— they tend to make people with a low self-esteem feel worse. Why? Because when we are weak in self-esteem, these claims are actually too contradictory to our existing beliefs. Interestingly, for one subset of people, optimistic affirmations work— those whose self-esteem is already high. Tweak them to make them more convincing for affirmations that work when your self-esteem is lagging behind. For example, "I'm going to be a huge hit, for starters! "I will persevere before I excel!"

2. Identify your competencies and develop them

Self-esteem is created by showing real potential and success in areas of our lives that matter to us. If you're proud to be a good cook so throw more dinner parties. If you're a good runner, log in and qualify for the runs. In brief, define your core competencies and find opportunities and jobs that prioritize them.

3. Learn to accept compliments

One of the trickiest facets of raising self-esteem is that we seem to be more prone to praise when we feel bad about ourselves— even though that is when we need them the most. And set yourself the objective of tolerating comments when you collect them even if they make you (and they'll) awkward. The best way to avoid the reflexive responses of batting away comments is to plan simple set replies and teach yourself to use them immediately whenever you get good feedback (e.g., "Thank you" or "How kind of you to say"). The tendency to reject or rebuff compliments will fade in time— which will also be a good sign that your self-esteem will grow stronger.

4. Eliminate self-criticism and introduce self-compassion

Unfortunately, by being self-critical, we are likely to damage it even more when our self-esteem is weak. Because our aim is to improve our self-esteem, self-criticism (which is almost always completely useless, even if it sounds compelling) needs to be replaced by self-compassion. Actually, as the self-critical inner monolog kicks in, ask yourself what you would say to a dear friend if they were in your position (we seem to be far more forgiving towards friends than we are towards ourselves) and apply those remarks to yourself. Doing so will discourage critical thoughts from undermining your self-esteem, and instead help build it up.

5. Affirm your real worth

The following technique has been shown to help revive your self-esteem after it has suffered a blow: Make a list of attributes that are important in the particular context. For starters, if you have been declined by your partner, list attributes that make you a good relationship candidate (e.g. being trustworthy or emotionally available); if you have struggled to get a job promotion, list qualities that make you a desirable employee (you have a strong work ethic or are responsible). Then choose one of the items on your list and write a short article (one or two paragraphs) on why other people are important and likely to enjoy the content in the future. Do the workout for a week every day, or whenever you need a lift of self-esteem.

The bottom line is enhancing self-esteem requires a bit of effort as it entails cultivating and sustaining healthy mental behaviors but doing so, and doing so properly, would deliver a great emotional and psychological return on your investment.

HOW TO IMPROVE YOUR DECISION MAKING

1. Cost-Benefit Analysis

Without reaching the final decision, it's necessary to weigh the pros and cons and make sure you make the best possible choice. It includes a cost-benefit analysis in which you analyze the result on any (positive and negative) path. This will help you see the cost of success, or the stuff you overlook when you choose one choice over another.

2. Narrow Your Options

For simplify the study of costs-benefits, restrict yourself for fewer options. When we are faced with more options, the greater the complexity of making a final decision. Further options will lead to more disappointment as we find all the missing opportunities and wonder if we could have selected one of the many other possible paths. Narrowing the options as such will result in better peace of mind.

3. Evaluate the Significance

How long would you wait mulling over a possible decision? Ten seconds to this? Ten minutes, right? 10 Days or more? It all depends on what is at stake. Determine the importance of a decision (How much of an impact will it have on my life? How much will it cost me?) to eliminate agonizing indecision, then set a deadline accordingly.

4. Don't Sweat the Small Stuff

If it is something as easy as choosing where to go for lunch or what to watch on tv, try to keep things in perspective and keep the decision-making time frame to a minimum. This is closely tied to determining the meaning of a decision— if it doesn't significantly affect you or others, then don't waste time arguing constantly about your choices.

5. Do Your Research

This may seem intuitive but when it comes to making major decisions — new cell phone or tablet, car brand, etc. — taking in the time and effort to thoroughly educate yourself about your future investment will mean the difference between product fulfillment and constant dissatisfaction.

6. Get a Well-Informed Opinion

It's more than just studying a decision's facts and details — having a personal opinion can also boost your decision making by giving you the confidence and reassurance that you're making the right choice. Whether it's telling your auto mechanic buddy before buying a car or reviewing Consumer Reports before buying a new kitchen appliance, informed opinions are really beneficial.

HOW TO EXERCISE YOUR BRAIN

1. Use all your senses

A research conducted in 2015 suggests using all the senses could help strengthen the brain.

Consider doing exercises that involve all five of your senses at the same time to give your senses and your brain a workout. You can try to bake a batch of cookies, visit a farmer's market, or try a new restaurant while you're focusing on smelling, touching, degusting, seeing and hearing all at once.

2. Learn a new skill

Not only is learning a new talent fun and interesting, it can also help reinforce the links within the brain.

Research from 2014 also suggests that learning a new ability in older adults will help to improve memory function.

You've always wanted to learn how to do something there? Maybe you want to learn how to fix your vehicle, use some software program or ride a horse? Now you've got another good reason to learn the new skill.

3. Teach a new skill to someone else

One of the best ways to extend your learning is to teach another person a talent.

You need to practice it after you have learned a new skill. This needs you to explain the concept to someone else, and correct any mistakes you make. Learn to swing a golf club for example and then show a friend the moves.

4. Listen to or play music

Want an easy way to boost your imaginative brain power? The solution may be to turn a music on.

Listening to positive melodies allows to create more innovative solutions, relative to being in silence, according to a 2017 report. That suggests, cranking up some feel-good music will help boost your creativity and creative thinking.

And if you want to learn how to play music, now is a great time to start, because at any point in your life, your brain is able to learn new things. That's why you're never too old to start playing a keyboard, guitar or even percussion instrument.

5. Take a new route

When it comes to your everyday tasks don't get stuck in a rut. Instead, be prepared to try out new ways of doing the same things.

Choose a different route to get to work every week or try another mode of transportation, such as walking or using public transportation instead of driving. A simple change will help your brain and you might be surprised at how easy it is to change your thinking.

6. Meditate

Meditation on a daily basis will relax the body, ease your breathing and reduce stress and anxiety.

But did you know it can also help to fine-tune your memory and improve the ability of your brain to process information?

Find a quiet spot, close your eyes and meditate for five minutes each day.

7. Learn a new language

A 2012 literature study showed unanimously the many cognitive advantages of being able to speak more than one language.

Bilingualism can lead to better memory, enhanced visual-spatial skills and higher levels of creativity, according to numerous studies. Also being fluent in more than one language will help you transition between different tasks more quickly, and delay the onset of mental decline due to ageing.

The good news is that reaping the benefits of learning a new language is never too late. According to experts, you can enhance your memory by becoming a student of a new language at any time in your life, and develop certain mental functions.

8. Take up tai chi

It's no secret that in many respects tai chi will help your fitness including your mental health. Plus, when life seems out of control, it can help stabilize you too.

Taking regular Tai Chi practice can help to reduce stress, improve the quality of sleep and improve memory. A research in 2013 showed that the long-term practice of tai chi could cause structural changes in the brain, leading to an increase in brain volume.

Beginners do their part by taking a class to master the various moves. But when you learn the fundamentals, you can practice tai chi anywhere, anywhere.

9. Focus on another person

If you communicate with someone every time you take care of four things about them. You may note their shirt or pants color.

Were they wearing spectacles? Have they got a hat on and if so, what kind of cap? What is their hair color?

If you plan to recall four things, make a mental note and then return to it later in the day. Write down what about those four specifics you recall.

HOW TO STOP NEGATIVE THINKING

1. Speak To The Negative Thought

Practice being aware of those feelings as they come up. Should you feel tired, thirsty, frustrated, depressed or anything else? We don't go anywhere as we try to ignore negative thoughts, we keep popping again. Recognize these to combat them. Let your inner voice say, "I hear a negative thought; it's a story that I'm telling myself and it's not real."

2. Get Around Positive People

Want to catch some cold? Get around with a cough, people. I'm not sure the suggestion really stands, but it does mean much to me when I mentor someone. I see many people associating with like-minded and often negative people as they try to change something, like a career, in their lives. Negatives aren't constructive. Physically get around positivity, through your ears and your pupils.

3. Don't Expect Everything To Be Perfect

It can be frustrating to expect everything to be flawless and it robs you of true happiness. Make sure that your dream of success really is steeped. Of eg, if you are elevated next year— as planned instead of this year— does one year really mean anything over the long term? Striving for goals trying to be flawless with a distance to the end state can be a refreshing way to live on your own terms.

4. Work With An Active Mindset

A bulletproof mentality is no alternative. It's important to discover a method that appeals for you. The group works better when teaching different types of clientele (executives, millennials and entrepreneurs). The one thing I found to be true and realistic is that no standard practice exists. Your attitude process is entirely tailored and will change based on what restricting values you are trying to remove, and what positive traits you are trying to instill in your daily routine. "Stick with it" is the most valuable advice I can give. Get into a routine, figure out what fits and don't hesitate until you've perfected the system you're using.

5. Develop A Positive Morning Routine

Early in the morning, thoughts begin. If the thought is controlled by a tyrant, they rule their life. Negative thinking will slow down a leader. Leaders have to captivate every thought by combining thoughts of terror with thoughts of hope and faith. One method that great thinkers use is to build a morning routine where they read something positive and encouraging every morning.

6. Just Breathe

You need to slow down everything to avoid negative thoughts, and first try to just note them. It will get you more comfort and self-awareness by integrating timers, alerts and actual time blocks into your life to just breathe. Then just breathe them out as you start noticing how many negative thoughts you're having. The key is not comparing yourself or getting caught up in the negative thoughts. Over time, you'll get better at this workout, just like anything else.

7. Become Intentional About Your Attitude

Having a positive attitude is a deliberate action starting as soon as you wake up in the morning. Be conscious as you concentrate on the negative, and make the decision to reflect instead on the positive. Your mindset reflects a decision. You draw what you're focused on so let go of something that doesn't match your interests. The more positive mind-shifts you do, the simpler that becomes.

8. Try The Displacement Theory

Have tried not thinking? Do it, and see what happens sometime. If you want to smash the habits of negative thinking, you have to replace them with something else. At the same moment, no-one can dream of two things. Now, pick something you'd love to do and start working on it; let your ideal project displace the old thoughts.

9. Focus On The Promise, Not The Problem

No matter what your abilities or current work environment are, if you let them live, there will always be grounds for negative thoughts. If you start feeling pessimistic, simply remember why you're there. Reflect on where you are going and why that matters to you. It's about the end goal though, not the difficult parts of the process.

10.   Tap Into The Root Problem

Often negative thinking arises from a problem not seen clearly on the table. I call it the "source question." Sometimes these destructive habits of thought are rooted in us from an early age and have become part of our culture. To transcend these destructive patterns of thought, you have to recognize the deeper-seeded explanation why these trends continue to show up. Then and only then can you tackle the problem.

11. Make A Conscious Choice

Unless you can expose what they are you can't get rid of negative thought patterns. Get to know the negative thoughts and how they get activated. Only with that self-awareness can you begin to identify when it occurs, and make a choice in the moment to change your focus.

WHAT IS EMPATHY HEALING?

Empathy heals. How? Have you ever been so tired, you could hardly get out of bed, but then someone got it right? I helped. It was your mate who brought broth. Her husband was making tea. Your mother called. They gave you drugs not. You have not even met you personally, but their compassion and empathy made you realize that you are not alone.

It can be a long and tough journey when you are recovering from something more than a cough. For the faint-hearted, detoxification is not. Mega successes (a month free of migraines!) can be interspersed with soothing emergencies (the worst of all earache). It is difficult to move about through fear and uncertainty. You can't eat what you used to want or maybe even do stuff that you used to love. Sitting alone with those defeats seems more like being robbed than advancing. It's easier to keep your eyes on the road ahead, with a traveling companion. Faith and hope can be harder to have. Partners don't just let partners withdraw by themselves. Neither parents nor kids do.

Healing a world bereft of empathy

Consider someone who doesn't feel safe in his or her body? Have you ever pondered this? Did you ever wonder how many people feel profoundly vulnerable inside the world?

They are a society devoid of empathy, and it is where society feels most about its lack of children; because the dysfunctional universe is as it is due to adults not fulfilling their emotional needs when they are young. They knew no idea what their emotions were and thus tried to hide them. The effect is a society full of people working under immense deprivation and suffering, which then negatively impacts the world when it is acting out. We maintain a dangerous world from a disembodied mind — from a state of inability to experience the pain, and thus occupy their body.

The intelligence is stronger because of the need for the victim to disassociate themselves from suffering into the mind of thought. Mentation is the location where hurtful, distorted bodies seek relief. Have you ever asked why reason favors Western civilization above emotions to the extent it does? This doesn't help the issue of persistent disembodiment from children to adults, of course. It's a vacillating circle. Ungrounded minds build and perpetuate Western dominant culture. It is run by strong, disembodied intellects, who are deeply afraid to feel. Which, as we can see, is highly dangerous.

The way to get out of the confusion is through. We're not fixing the universe by altering what's "out there;" instead, we're curing it by gradually leaning into what our minds have long resisted.

The world desperately needs people who live out a profound sense of security. A sense of comfort internally fosters a drive to build stability for others and our world. A balanced biology makes safer, life-giving decisions because the thinking-mind is in sync with the body-feel. We do not work independently but as a cohesive network, perceiving life as a single whole.

Healing is the transition from one part to the next. We initiate this process by re-inhabiting the pieces of ourselves that we have long suppressed— the emotions.

The earth heals as we heal, as we give the tired, uncomfortable feelings in our bodies long-awaited empathy; as we approach the delicate human body of our and others as we would a young child — with concern, with a sensitive ear, with a need to be with and sooth.

CONCLUSION

You have come so far to read all of this. It's a surprise how driven you have to be so committed to fixing your outlook and making yourself a happier person. First and foremost I hope you will be able to bring yourself to be congratulated. Beat yourself on the head, sit back and be proud, but you see fit— the most important thing about breaking a pattern of negative thinking is that it doesn't apply to those who only ask others for assistance without doing much about themselves. The only way you can live a better and more meaningful existence is if you can put out your hand and do it yourself. You have to be the one to take the perfect first step towards recovery and strengthening and that's just what you're doing. That's a really admirable thing to do, so I'm sincerely confident you can be proud of making a move forward.

That's another very widespread form of slowly chipping away from your self-deprecation habits — thinking of good things, even the smallest of things. No matter how small you might think it is, no matter how meaningless you might think something you have done is, I would like to congratulate you and do it well. We take this sort of thing so often absolutely for granted, actually. Some activities we do during our morning or evening rituals are so often disregarded. When we get so wrapped up on the things we do wrong, we sometimes find it hard to remember and document the stuff that we do well every single day. When that happens, just take a step back for a moment. Curiously, temporary isolation can be a good idea, though with few and far between times of that detachment, if your negative thinking is particularly unhealthy or dangerous. Take a step back and simply understand that the things you are doing well far outweigh the things you are doing wrong. You'll know even those things that you're still doing incorrectly. That is another thing about us that's crazy — we're learning things. Yet, more often than not, we are really learning things, very quickly. It's a strange thing, but when we start something new we get so caught up in what we can't do yet that we somehow lose the ability to tell what we can do now. Many people say this way of sorting out what we can and can't do, and dwelling on the category "can't," is heavily related to our growth. If you were an animal focused solely on life, you should concentrate on what you have yet to discover, rather than what you already learned. But-in this situation you are not in a position to dwell on that sort of thing. In fact, sometimes we learned how to reflect on our shortcomings and the stuff we haven't accomplished just yet in a positive way that helps us to learn more easily. Then, we began learning how to look at our shortcomings and those mysterious talents not with constructive criticism, but rather with a negative

150

hand. Today, some of us can't help but look at a list of things we really can't do and we feel like we're sad. Because of what kind of world you grew up in, if you are reading this book and connected to at least some of the stuff you've done, you're definitely someone who, as a teenager, had a lot of pressure on you. This burden is hurting and I'm sorry. The burden of trying to surprise your friends or peers with your good grades too badly, feeling upset with yourself when you don't live up to their expectations, the pain you get in bed late that night, worrying about all the things you might easily have done just a little better. If you'd just been working a bit harder; a bit more often if you'd just paid a little more interest in the class the day before. It's awful to feel like you have failed the people you care for, and want to be the most proud of you. Live with the remorse of what you know is making those men, those role models, unhappy in you, is something I would never want for anyone because I do honestly recognize the emotion, I like to think. If you're reading this, you may never have conquered the shame about letting down your parents and teachers, so you've continued to try. You kept trying and you were busy for years and years trying to satisfy them. Maybe as you grew older their standards increased, and with them you were forced to grow faster and faster. You may have lost a little bit of your youth to that addiction and now you like that obsession a little bit of your adult. It hurts feeling like you are doomed to fail them no matter what you do. I understand the pain.

Please know that, no matter what happens today, people will always be proud of you. You should be proud of yourself, above all. For so long, you've come so far and done so much for yourself, suffering and fighting tooth and nail just to keep up with peers. That's why, on the one hand, you have done what you have. The fascination has made you grow up to be competent and acclimatized to stressful environments in a macabre way. On the other hand, doing just that and tempering your competitive spirit has not only exercised your intellect and helped you to deal with stress, anxiety and other people's expectations, but has done the opposite in the process as well. While it made you become more competitive, it pulled you down until you didn't have to be competitive any more. When there were no more expectations for you to follow in school or at home, you were left with that obsessive nature that guided you to always do well and to ignore everything that you had already achieved. Yet, you had to make tough expectations of your own. It was tough but I think you will take a step back to realize how far you have come on your path. You have, after all, come so amazingly fast. See you. Love yourself.

CPSIA information can be obtained
at www.ICGtesting.com
Printed in the USA
BVHW061006040321
601713BV00012B/1037